Puberty
Unplugged

Steve Barlow
and
Steve Skidmore

Illustrations by Stuart Harrison

Kingfisher

Kingfisher
An imprint of Larousse plc
Elsley House,
24-30 Great Titchfield Street,
London W1P 7AD

First published by Larousse plc 1996

10 9 8 7 6 5 4 3 2 1

A CIP catalogue record for this book is available from
the British Library.

ISBN 0 7534 0032 4

Printed and bound in Great Britain

Designed by Val Carless

Contents

Chapter 1
All Change Please 5

Chapter 2
Hairy Bits 11

Chapter 3
Breasts 18

Chapter 4
Boys' Bits 23

Chapter 5
Girls' Bits 28

Chapter 6
Periods & Reproduction 32

Chapter 7
Hygiene 49

Chapter 8
Diet & Exercise 60

Chapter 9
Emotions & other Pressures 66

Chapter 10
Sex 78

Helplines 95

Index 96

Introduction

by Nick Fisher

Childhood is like a warm bath. It's years of comfortable fun splashing and playing, with no real worries. Then along comes puberty and yanks the plug out of your childhood. With a bit of useful help and guidance you can get out while the water's still hot. Left to yourself, you might end up sitting there damp and shivering, wondering what to do next.

Puberty can cause such confusion because so much gets crammed into such a small period of time. Your body changes, your emotions change, your friends change, your mind develops. There's more happening inside and outside your body than ever before in your life. But, at the same time, you're supposed to sit school exams, make academic decisions that could affect you for years, navigate through friendships and relationships, separate from your parents' influence and learn to act like an adult.

Puberty can feel a bit like being parachuted into the centre of a hostile foreign city without a map. You could stop people and ask for help to find your way out. But you don't necessarily have the language or want to draw attention to yourself. Yet if you had your own guidebook, you'd definitely do it more easily. That's not to say you still won't make the odd wrong turn. But at least when you reach the occasional dead end, you'll have some information to set you back on the right road.

Puberty Unplugged is just that – a guidebook to help you pick your way through the back alleys of your teens. Even if it hasn't got all the answers, it can help you ask the right questions.

Chapter 1

All Change Please

Over the centuries many stupid and ill-informed things have been written and said about growing up.

Daft Dick Says...

It's best to grow up at an early age.

FASCINATING FACTS

Adolescence is taken from the Latin word *adolescere*, which means to grow up. *Pubertas* is not the name of a Brazilian footballer. It is the Latin word meaning adulthood. So now you know where puberty comes from.

In fact, it doesn't matter when puberty begins. There isn't anything wrong with being an early or a late developer.

Girls can reach puberty any time between the ages of 8 and 17. Boys get there any time between 10 and 18.

TALLER GIRLS

Girls begin their spurt for growth at an earlier age than boys. This means that for a few months, girls tend to be taller than boys.

SQUEAKY CLEAN

During puberty, a boy's voice gets lower and deeper than a girl's. This is because a man has a larger voice box (larynx) than a woman. Take a look at the size of a boy's Adam's apple and see how much more it sticks out than a girl's.

When the larynx muscles develop during puberty, a boy's voice breaks. This is why his voice crackles all over the place, deep and booming one second, piping and squeaking the next.

Change

MALE

- Get taller
- Grow broader shoulders
- Chest gets broader
- Muscle growth
- Voice gets deeper
- Face will change shape
- Could get spots
- Feet and hands get bigger
- Facial hair grows
- Body hair grows
- Pubic hair grows
- Penis and testicles get bigger

What can you look forward to when puberty strikes? Suddenly, you're not the person you used to be...

Chart...

FEMALE

- Get taller
- Face will change shape
- Could get spots
- Breasts grow
- Feet and hands get bigger
- Hips get wider
- Body hair grows
- Pubic hair grows
- Facial hair grows
- The vulva develops
- Ovaries develop
- Periods begin

All of this to do! And you've got to try and keep up with what's happening in the soap operas, do your schoolwork, play sports, tidy your bedroom and have some sort of a social life. How will you fit it all in? Puberty can be a busy and stressful time!

7

HORROR MOANS

Your body begins to develop because of chemical substances called *hormones*. They should more accurately be called Horror Moans!

Why? Because they'll make you moan in horror when you look in a mirror! And unfortunately, this moaning can go on for several years!

OH MY GOD, I'VE GOT A ZIT ON MY NOSE AND I'M SUPPOSED TO BE GOING TO A PARTY!

YOUR QUESTIONS ANSWERED

Our tip-top, hot-shot, health-helper Dr Ivel*, is here to answer all your questions about hormones.

What are hormones, anyway?

Well, they're chemical substances produced in humans, plants and animals. Sometimes they're called chemical messengers because they cause various reactions in the body.

So where do these hormones come from?

In humans, hormones are produced in the endocrine glands. From here they get sent out all over the body via the bloodstream.

* Oh – all right then, Dr Ivel doesn't exist. It's really us and we're not doctors, but we've read loads of books about puberty (well, one or two) – and we've almost grown-up ourselves!

HOW DOES ALL THIS HORMONE BUSINESS BEGIN?

1 The hypothalamus gland – that's the one in the brain – begins to grow.

2 When the hypothalamus has grown, it starts beaming out hormones to the pituitary gland, located conveniently nearby in the brain.

3 The hormones from the hypothalamus kick-start the pituitary into action. The pituitary gets busy pumping out massive quantities of two other hormones called FSH and LH. For those brainboxes among you who are into long words, these letters stand for *Follicle Stimulating Hormone* and *Luteinizing Hormone*. Well, you did ask!

4 FSH and LH wing their way all around the body in the blood, then get to grips with your sexual organs – they're the ones you can blame for all the bother that lies ahead. FSH and LH stimulate the growth of ova in girls' ovaries and sperm in boys' testes.

5 As if that wasn't enough, the ovaries and testes now start to release their own hormones. Girls produce oestrogen and progesterone. Boys produce testosterone. These are the hormones responsible for all the changes that take place during puberty.

INTERESTING FACTS

The ovaries produce low levels of male hormones. The testes produce low levels of female hormones.

MORE HORROR MOANS

Hormones are also produced in the thyroid gland (in the neck), in the kidneys, and in the intestine! Not all hormones are to do with sex. Read on...

Cortisol and corticosteroide
● Help the body to cope with pain and shock. ● Boost levels of glucose in the body when needed. ● Help control fat levels in the body.

Adrenaline and noradrenaline
● Prepare the body for sudden activity.

Prolactin
● Controls milk supply in breast-feeding women. ● Helps in the production of female sex hormones.

Thyroxine
● Speeds up chemical reactions in the body.

Insulin
● Controls sugar levels in the blood.

EYE-WATERING FACT

If you wanted to stop a boy developing into a man, the way to do it would be to remove his testicles before the male hormones could be produced. This is known as castration.

Don't read the following if you are of a nervous disposition!

This is how the Romans castrated kids:

"...children still of a tender age are placed in a vessel of hot water, and then when the parts are softened in the bath, the testicles are to be squeezed with the fingers until they disappear...."
Paulus Aegineta OUCH!

10

Chapter 2

Hairy Bits

LET'S HEAR IT FOR HAIR
During puberty you will find that hair suddenly starts sprouting up on various parts of your body.

Apparently, this is all to do with the past when we were apes and covered head-to-toe in hair to keep us warm.* Again, it's those fun-filled sex hormones that cause our body hair to sprout.

* We mean in the days before jeans, bra tops, T-shirts and micro minis were invented.

THE BIG QUESTION

How much hair is going to grow on me?

This really depends on how hairy your parents are! Your genes will determine how much hair you will have. If you are dark-haired, the hair will show up more than if you are fair-haired.

If you are this hairy, you are either a dog or a werewolf. If you are a werewolf, it is important to avoid silver bullets and be wary of full moons. If you are a dog and reading this, alert the media immediately, as you will probably earn enough money to keep you in dog biscuits and choc-drops for the rest of your canine life. If you are a human and you think you are a dog, get medical help – and get it *FAST!*

Where Hair

Puberty is a hair-raising time – hair suddenly starts raising all over the place!

FASCINATING FACTS

It is common for pubic hair to be a different colour from the hair on your head?

Pubic hair

This grows around your genitals (yes, the bits between your legs). Your pubic hair is soft at first, but as you age, it will become fuzzier and coarser. Pubic hair can also be found in your bed in the morning – and usually on bars of soap in the bathroom!

Grows...

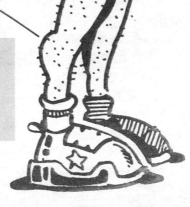

Underarm hair
We don't know for sure what purpose underarm hair has, but it's going to grow there, so get used to the idea!

Fashion hint
Wigs and toupées around this area are a no-no – they are definitely not trendy.

Arm and leg hair
In general, body hair shows up more on men because their hair is coarser.

Hairdresser's tips
You don't need to perm your pubic hair. Dandruff is not usually a problem either.

Beards and moustaches

Usually, one of the last things that happens during puberty for boys, is that hair grows on the face.

Like pubic hair, it starts out soft and then grows coarser. At about the time when you're sprouting your first proud facial hairs, fun-loving and totally sensitive dads and male teachers will make some hilarious comments about your bumfluff. (They don't mean fluff growing out of your bottom.) This jokey (ha ha!) way of referring to your beard is all part of the joy of growing up. The best way to deal with such witty comments is to put on a brave smile, stick one finger up, and tell the jolly joker: "Up yours, grandad."*

* On second thoughts, don't say this, as it could result in detentions and/or being grounded for the next million years, by which time your 'bumfluff' will have grown past your bum and down to the floor.

PS It's also common for girls to have fine hair growing on their face, and it's more noticeable if your hair is dark. If you are very unhappy about it, the worst thing to do is to shave, because it will only grow back bristly. You can use a hair-removing cream or special bleach cream. Probably your best bet is to go to a beauty salon and have the hair removed professionally.

Gardening tips

Topiary is the art of cutting hedges into interesting shapes. The same can be done for pubic hair!*
* We don't know of many people who have actually done this, but we think it's a brilliant idea. It could be a whole new art form!

14

THE HAIRY CHEST

Not all males have hair growing on their chest, but some do. Some also have it on their stomach, shoulders, arms, legs, hands and feet. Some have it on their back, too.

Daft Dick Says...

The more hair you've got, the more manly you are. . .

. . . No, the more hair you've got, the more money you'll have to spend on shampoo! It doesn't matter if you have swathes of jungle-thick hair carpeting your body from head to foot or none at all. Hair has nothing to do with 'manliness' – whatever that means!

REMOVING HAIR

Some women like to remove the hair on their legs and under their arms for reasons of fashion or culture. There's no reason why you should do this – it's purely a matter of choice.

If you are going to remove body hair, you can use a razor or a hair-removing cream (depilatory). Waxing is also an alternative, but it can be painful and expensive. Sugaring is like waxing, but it's something you can do at home with a kit. One of the latest ways of getting rid of unwanted hair is to use an epilator. This is like a razor, but it plucks out the hairs rather than cutting them off. You get brilliant results, but it's absolute agony! Some girls also remove pubic hair around their 'bikini line'. Be especially careful when doing this, as the skin there is particularly sensitive!

SHAVING

Shaving doesn't make you a man. In fact the sooner you begin to shave, the more time you're going to have to waste standing in front of a mirror when you could be out enjoying yourself!

The easiest and quickest way to shave is to use an electric razor. However, many people prefer a 'wet and foam' shave, because they get a closer, smoother shave.

Daft Dick Says...

The sooner you shave, the sooner you're a man.

SWEENY TODD'S TIPS

- Use a safety razor to avoid cutting your throat.
- Use short strokes of the razor.
- Let the razor glide over your skin – remember you're not trying to peel an onion!
- If you have sensitive skin, use a shaving foam or gel for sensitive skins. Use an after-shaving balm rather than aftershave, which can dry out the skin (and really sting)!
- If you do cut yourself,* stick on a bit of loo roll to stop the bleeding. There are also sticks you can buy.
- Don't use anyone else's razor – you might pick up an infection.
- Change your razor blade frequently – blunt blades cut you!

* Sorry, this should read WHEN you cut yourself!

FASCINATING FACTS

It is thought that early man used seashells, flints and sharks' teeth in order to achieve that perfect shave.

King Camp Gillette patented the safety razor in 1895 and they are still going strong.

16

SAFE SHAVING

Follow this safe step-by-step guide to wet shaving and you'll avoid looking like Vincent Van Gogh,* who could never wear spectacles again.

1. Soak your face with warm water. Don't overdo this stage.

2. Put foam or gel on face. Don't overdo this stage either.

3. Start to shave from one ear and work down to your chin.

4. Find out that you forgot to pick up the razor.

5. Pick up razor.

6. Start shaving from one ear and work down to your chin, ensuring that you have the razor the right way around.

7. Rinse off excess foam and hairs from razor as you work your way down.

8. Scream AARRRGHHHHH! when you realize that you have cut yourself.

9. Go to other ear. Follow steps 6 and 7.

10. Swear very loudly when you realize that you have repeated step 8 as well.

11. Shave your top lip and under your chin.

12. Rinse off traces of foam.

13. Splash face with cold water – this closes up the pores.

14. Splash on aftershave.

15. Cry as the aftershave gets into all the cuts.

16. Stick pieces of loo roll on the cuts.

17. Think seriously about growing a beard.

* He chopped off his ear.

17

Chapter 3

Breasts

You'll love them or hate them,
but they're all yours.

WHAT ARE BREASTS FOR?

A) To give moronic males a chance to shout
"Cor pheweee take a look at them!"

B) To act as a secondary sexual feature.

C) To help you get a part on Baywatch.

D) To produce milk for feeding a baby.

Answers b and d are correct.

(Although a and c may also apply, these are not the
biological functions of breasts!)

THANKS FOR THE MAMMARY

Breasts are mammary glands. This word comes from the name for all warm blooded animals – mammals. All female mammals have mammary glands, which secrete milk developed during pregnancy for the feeding of their young off-spring.

FASCINATING FACTS

In Victorian times, a supposedly foolproof method to increase breast size was to bathe in twenty pounds of fresh strawberries.

Grow your own breasts

Grow Your Oan Breasts

- Take your body.
- Let it age for a few years.
- Do nothing special, except enjoy yourself – and do your schoolwork! Oh, yes – and a few odd jobs around the house.
- When your body is ready, the ovaries will release oestrogen.
- Still you need do nothing!
- Your nipples and the skin around them (called the areola) sometimes get darker.
- Your nipples may also begin to stand up.
- Still – do nothing!
- Before you know it, your breasts will begin to grow. (You may not even notice it at first.)
- They may feel sore and tender – don't worry, this is perfectly normal and will soon stop.
- One breast may grow more quickly than the other. *DON'T WORRY!* This is normal, and they usually even up in size. In most cases, the breasts will reach their full size by the time you are 18.
- To help support your breasts, you may wish to wear a bra (short for brassière – see page 22).

SO HOW DO THEY GROW?

Well, it's thanks to those good old hormones again. In fact, it's the female hormone, oestrogen (produced by the ovaries) that causes breasts to grow. OK, we heard you – you want to know how breasts grow. It's dead easy! Just check out the following guide to growing your own breasts!

BREAST BREAKDOWN

There are more to your breasts than meets the eye!

Nipples

Nipples can be different shapes. They can be turned inwards as well as outwards. The nipple is the most sensitive part of the breast. It can stand erect when touched or if you get very cold. There are microscopic holes in the nipple, which allow milk to come out when a baby sucks on it.

Alveoli

When a woman has a baby, milk is made in these leaf-like structures.

Lactiferous ducts (or milk ducts)

There are between 15 and 20 ducts in each breast. In a child, these are very small, but at puberty they start to grow. When a woman becomes pregnant and produces milk for her baby, the milk passes from the alveoli along these ducts and out through the nipple.

Fat

This protects the milk ducts.

The areola

This is the dark skin that surrounds the nipple. There are tiny lumps in the areola – these are glands. They produce a fluid that helps to lubricate the nipple when a mother feeds her baby. Hairs sometimes grow from the areola – if you wish to, you can cut them off. The areola gets darker as a woman grows older, or if she gets pregnant.

Fibres

These separate the milk ducts. The fibres are like elastic and stretch as you get older. This can make the breasts droop.

Some scientists believe that enlarged breasts developed in the human female as a sex signal, as the size of a woman's breasts does not relate to the amount of milk that she can produce. Perhaps this is why some girls can be very sensitive about the appearance of their boobs.

Just as boys worry about the size of their willies, girls can worry about the size of their breasts. Are they too big or too small?

The simple fact is that there's no such thing as an 'ideal' size. Our ideal seems to come from images of 'perfect' bodies that appear in the media. In the 17th, 18th and 19th centuries the favourite models of painters were curvacious, large-breasted women.

In the 1920s – the age of the flappers – flat-chested women were supposed to be beautiful.

In recent times some women have had silicone implants to boost the size of their boobs, while others starve themselves until their boobs disappear, trying to look like supermodels.

The secret is to realize that fashion is fickle, and has little relation to real-life everyday women. Be positive about your breasts, whatever their size!

"I must, I must increase my bust!"

Exercise can't help you increase the size of your bust. Exercise helps you build up muscle – but breasts are mostly made of fat, not muscle. It is the amount of fat in your breasts that determines how large they are.

BRAS

Do you need to wear a bra? It's up to you!

PS

If you want to wear a bra, don't feel embarrassed about telling your parents – although you might get an interesting reply if you are a boy!

BRA SIZE

Bras come in many sizes.

The first thing to do when buying a bra is to measure your chest. Measure underneath your breasts around the ribcage – then add 12 cm.

Next, find out your cup size. Measure around the fullest part of your breasts. If it's the same as your chest measurement, you're an A cup. If it's 2.5 cm bigger, you're a B cup. If it's 5 cm bigger, you're C cup, and so on.

Probably the best way to choose a bra is to try on lots of different types until you find one you like the look of and which feels comfortable. Go to a shop with a wide selection, from stretch and sport's bras to glamorous underwired models.

Enjoy yourself!

Chapter 4

Boys' Bits

*Boys' breasts also develop during puberty!
But before all you male readers rush off to look
in a mirror or buy a bra, we should point out that
your breasts won't develop like a girl's!*

What might happen:

- Your nipples might get larger.
- Your areolae might get darker and wider.
- Your breasts might get lumps under them.
- They might feel sore.
- They might swell.

BUT, even if all these things happen, you aren't going to grow a pair of breasts and turn into a girl so don't panic!

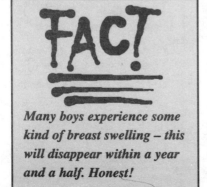

Many boys experience some kind of breast swelling – this will disappear within a year and a half. Honest!

WILLIES

Boys have a very close attachment to their penises – sometimes even giving them their own special nickname! Apart from its official name, the penis is also known as: willy, winkle, one-eyed trouser snake, dick, sausage, chipolata, truncheon, member, tackle, cock, knob, prick, dong, long john, donger, tool, weapon, wanger, john thomas, organ, chopper, dagger, lance, tool, rod, pork sword, stick, joystick, staff of life, wriggling pole, mad mick, boner, peenie, weenie, jigger, crank, ding-a-ling, ferret, pink oboe, blue-veined piccolo, plonker, man-root, worm, third leg, middle stump, horn, pizzle, private, plaything, jock, jammy, end, woofer, ying, yang and yutz.

SO WHAT'S IT ALL ABOUT?

When puberty hits boys, they soon know about it because their sex organs start to grow. First, your testes get bigger. Then, around a year later, your penis grows. Don't worry about one testicle getting bigger than the other – by the time you reach adulthood, they'll have evened up in size!

When you are young your penis has only one function – you pee through it. But once puberty begins and the sex hormones start developing and surging through your body, another function develops. Yes, your penis can help you make babies.

When a man gets sexually excited, blood flows into the penis and it begins to stick out and up – it gets erect. This happens in order for it to be able to penetrate inside a woman's vagina and so help to produce babies (see page 91).

Apart from this practical function, the willy is an organ that will give you a lifetime of pleasure – as long as you look after it and use it sensibly and with respect!

DO I MEASURE UP?

Most males – perhaps even all of them – worry about the size of their penis. They think that the bigger it is, the better lovers they will make, and the more girls will fancy them. If they have a small one, they feel it somehow makes them 'less manly'. This is nonsense – size is immaterial.

Daft Dick says...

The bigger your willy, the more of a man you are.
The bigger your willy, the better lover you will be.
If you've got big feet, you've got a big willy.
WRONG!

Myths about the penis could probably fill several libraries. They stem from a lack of knowledge and the fact that the majority of teenage boys – and even grown men – are too scared or embarrassed to talk TRUTHFULLY about their willies.

SOME WILLY FACTS

- The average length of a limp penis is between 5 and 11 cm.
- The average length of an erect penis is between 12.5 and 17.5 cm. But look at the chart opposite.
- Very few men have a penis bigger or smaller than this.
- A small penis does not make any difference to male or female sexual pleasure.
- Having a big willy does not make you more of a man or a better lover!

So keep cool, and keep it in perspective. Even if you think you're well endowed, here's something to put you in your place – the blue whale's penis is over 3 m long! That takes some beating!

SIZE CHART??

0 cm
Either you're a girl, or you're holding the book the wrong way round.

0 - 3 cm	Normal
3 - 6 cm	Normal
6 - 9 cm	Normal
9 - 12 cm	Normal
12 - 16 cm	Normal
16 - 19 cm	Normal
19 - 22 cm	Normal

Off the page
Possibly you are a compulsive liar!

A CUT ABOVE THE REST?

In some cultures it is common for the foreskin to be removed for reasons of religion, hygiene or tradition. This is called circumcision. Jewish boys have their foreskins removed 8 days after they are born. There are no real advantages or disadvantages in having, or not having a foreskin.

in   cm
7   18
      17
      16
6   15
      14
5   13
      12
      11
4   10
       9
       8
3   7
       6
2   5
       4
       3
1
       2

       1

Sizing it up...

Worried about the size of your willy?

- Use this liar's ruler.
- Measure your willy. (Don't do this in a public place or at the dinner table.)
- Record the figure.
- Boast to your friends about how big your willy is.
- Then realize that you are a total plonker!

Now you know where your bits and pieces are, let's find out what they're called.

Sperm ducts
Two tubes about 40 cm long connect the epididymis and the urethra.

LOADSASPERM!
An adult's testes produce 15,000 sperm every 5 seconds! Phew!

Glans
This is the sensitive tip of the penis.

Foreskin
The fold of skin that covers the glans is called the foreskin. It glides smoothly over the glans, helped by a whitish jelly-like juice called smegma. Stale smegma can build up under the foreskin and cause a pretty nasty smell or even an infection. So it's very important to wash regularly under the foreskin to keep it clean and healthy.

Penis
The penis is usually small and soft. It becomes erect when a male is sexually excited. More blood flows into it, making it larger and harder.

The ruler on the left side reads (top to bottom): in / cm, 9 / 26, 25, 24, 8 / 23, 22, 21, 7 / 20, 19, 18, 6 / 17, 16, 15, 5 / 14, 13, 12, 4 / 11, 10, 3 / 9, 8, 7, 2 / 6, 5, 4, 1 / 3, 2, 1

BOYS' BITS AND PIECES

Seminal vesicles

These two glands produce a fluid that helps nourish the sperm.

Testes or balls

Every day your testes produce several million male sex cells called sperm, as well as the sex hormone testosterone. Sperm take about two months to become fully formed. They can only thrive at a lower temperature than body heat. This is why your testes hang outside your body. It would be too hot for them to be inside the body like a girl's ovaries.

SWING ALONG

The left testis usually hangs lower than the right. This helps you to run and walk comfortably without them banging into each other and causing total agony!

Scrotum

This is the 'carrier bag' that holds the testes outside the body where sperm can happily be produced. When your testes are too cold, they shrink back towards the warmth of your groin. This is why your scrotum looks like a small walnut when you get out of a swimming pool or stand in a cold shower. It's just the body's way of trying to warm up your testes!

Epididymis

This is a coiled tube that lies on each testis. If you unravelled the tube it would measure over 6 m!* The sperm travel from the testes to the epididymis where they stay for about 2 weeks before travelling on to the sperm ducts.

* We strongly recommend that you do NOT try to unravel your epididymis. Or anyone else's for that matter.

Urethra

This has two functions:
1. It carries urine from the bladder out of the body.
2. It carries semen through the penis.

Semen is a mixture of sperm and the fluids produced by the seminal vesicles and prostate gland.

Prostate gland

This gland also produces a fluid. It helps the sperm to swim easily along the urethra.

Chapter 5

Girls' Bits

Girls' bodies change dramatically during puberty – it's all quite exciting!

THE INSIDE STORY

So this is what it all looks like... Read on to find out how all the bits work together – it's quite amazing!

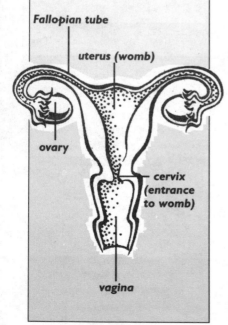

Fallopian tube

uterus (womb)

ovary

cervix (entrance to womb)

vagina

DARK SECRETS

Most female sex organs are INSIDE the body. This is the reason why girls feel more private about their sex organs than boys do. Whereas boys have to handle their willies all the time to pee, and while peeing they get to look at their own willies and those of other boys, girls' bodies are naturally more discreet. Girls pee on their own and tend to be more private about being seen naked. What's more, they can only look at their own most private parts with the help of a mirror.

FASCINATING FACTS

The Latin name for the female genitals is vulva. It means opening. Labia is the Latin word for lips.

GIRLS' BITS AND PIECES

Here is a guide to the different bits that make up the female genitalia.

Clitoris

The clitoris is a small lump at the front of the vulva. Although not very big, the clitoris is full of nerve endings, which makes it the most sensitive part of the female body. The tip of the clitoris has a fold of skin over it. Like a man's penis, the size of the clitoris varies from person to person.

Mons

This mound of fat protects the pubic bone. Pubic hair grows over it.

Vaginal opening

This is the entrance to the vagina. The vagina leads to the sex organs that are inside a woman's body. Blood comes out of the vaginal opening during a period. It is also through this small opening that babies leave the body when they are born. Don't worry! The opening stretches massively during childbirth! The vaginal opening is also where a man puts his penis during sex.

Inner labia

These have no hair on them. They are bright pink and moist, like the inside of your mouth, and sometimes protrude a little from the vulva.

Outer labia

These two thick folds of skin protect the vulva. The outer labia usually have pubic hair growing on them.

Hymen

This is a thin layer of skin that partly covers the opening to the vagina. Not all girls are born with a hymen. It has small holes in it to allow blood to pass through during a period.

Anus

This is where faeces leave your body through the alimentary canal.

Urethra

The urethra is a tube connecting the bladder to the outside of the body. Urine leaves the body through the urinary opening.

HYMEN INTACT

In the old days it was thought that if the hymen was broken it meant that a girl had had sex and was no longer a virgin. In fact, it is far more likely that the hymen will be broken during exercise than sex – especially exercise that involves lots of stretching, such as gymnastics, and cycling or horseriding. Sometimes the hymen breaks without you realizing it.

As any newly-born baby will tell you, the womb is specially kitted out to give the foetus the very best start in life, from being an egg to its birthday.

WHAT IS AN OVUM EXACTLY?

Ovum is the Latin word for egg. An ovum is a single egg cell. Ova is the plural of ovum.

FASCINATING FACTS

The place where your pubic hair grows – the 'mons' or soft flesh that covers your pubic bone – is nicknamed the 'mound of Venus' after the Roman goddess of love.

FEMALE REPRODUCTIVE ORGANS

Ovaries

These glands are about the size of a thumbnail. They are attached to the uterus by the fallopian tubes. When a girl is born she will have between one and two million ova in her ovaries. When you reach puberty, a single ovum is released every month from one of your two ovaries.

Fallopian tubes

These are also called uterine tubes. The two muscular tubes are between 7 - 13 cm long. When an ovum is released it passes along the tube towards the uterus.

Uterus

The uterus is also called the womb. It looks a little like an upside-down pear, and is made of muscles that can stretch enormously. If a woman gets pregnant, a baby will grow in the uterus.

Vagina

This is a muscular tube 8 -10 cm long. It connects the uterus to the outside of the body. It is extremely elastic so that a baby can be born through it. There are glands in the lining of the vagina. They secrete a lubricating and cleansing fluid.

Cervix

This is the entrance to the uterus. Although it looks very narrow, when a woman gives birth the cervix stretches enormously to allow the baby to pass through it. If the cervix couldn't stretch like this, all babies would be extremely long and thin!

Chapter 6

Periods & Reproduction

IMPORTANT!!!
BOYS, READ THIS SECTION!

PERIODS? WHO'D HAVE THEM?

Well, no one actually *wants* periods, but girls usually have them every 28 days. Periods are one of the most important changes for a girl during puberty. They show that her body is able to conceive a baby.

As with all the other changes in puberty, a girl's periods will begin when her body decides it's ready. Usually, periods start a year or two after her breasts or nipples have begun to develop.

In the old days it was thought embarrassing to talk about periods, and some people still find it difficult. If adults have trouble explaining periods to girls, it's no wonder that boys aren't told much about them either – after all, boys don't have

them! This acute lack of knowledge can lead to males having some very strange ideas!

When lads get together and talk about girls and periods, they can make dorkish jokes, giggle stupidly, tease girls and generally try and show off to their friends. However, the sad truth is that adolescent boys don't usually understand much about girls and how their bodies work. But they should. Because when they realize why and how periods happen, they will be able to understand better how girls are feeling and why they act in certain ways. This can make boys more considerate and understanding towards the female sex! And that can mean girls like them a lot better.
So boys, read on!

WHAT IS A PERIOD?

It's a monthly bleeding from the vagina. The blood comes when the lining of the uterus breaks down.

HOW OFTEN DO THEY HAPPEN?

Most women have a period every 28 days. This is known as a menstrual cycle. The cycle can vary from anything between 20 to 35 days. Some women do not have regular periods, especially when they first begin. This doesn't mean there is anything wrong. It's quite normal to wait 6 months or even a year between your first and second periods!

WHEN DO PERIODS START?

This can happen any time between the ages of 9 and 18.

HOW LONG DOES A PERIOD LAST?

It's usually over after 4 or 5 days. But sometimes it might last for just a couple of days, and other times it could go on for 8 days.

HOW MUCH BLOOD IS LOST?

This varies amongst women. Usually it's only a couple of tablespoons of blood each time, though it can feel like gallons! The blood is mixed with other fluids and cells from inside the uterus (the womb).

DO PERIODS HURT?

Unfortunately, they can. Many women suffer period pains. These are aching pains or cramps in the belly. It is thought that they're caused by hormones that make the uterus contract (squeeze up). Sometimes exercise and gentle stretching can help the muscles to relax. But if periods are particularly painful, it may be best to take a painkiller and lie down in a warm place. A hot-water bottle placed against the belly or in the small of the back may be comforting. If the pain is severe and continues, it would be a good idea to see your doctor.

DO PERIODS LAST ALL YOUR LIFE?

No, they don't. A woman will stop having periods around age 45 to 55. This is called the menopause or 'change of life'.

The medical term for having a period is menstruation. This comes from the Latin word mensis, which means month.

SHARK ATTACK!

Periods are also known as being: on, on the rag, coming on, the curse, wrong time of the month, on the blob, a monthly, and (euphemistically) my friend. Two quaint Australian terms for periods are shark attack! and surfing the crimson wave!

FASCINATING FACTS

Over a hundred years ago, the average age for a girl to begin her period was 16. Today the average age for periods to begin is 12. This is because people nowadays tend to be much healthier and eat a better diet.

PERIODS AND RELIGION

Some girls in Sikh, Hindu and Islamic cultures have to follow certain rules when they begin their periods. Sikh girls are expected to change the way they dress when they reach puberty. A muslim girl may have to have a ritual bath after her period has finished. This is called a *ghusi*. In some parts of Africa women are banned from cooking or picking crops while they are menstruating. In some places women are even banned from leaving their home!

DYSMENORRHOEA

What is it?

a) An explosive case of diarrhoea.
b) A Welsh cake made from seaweed.
c) The name of a Russian shotputter.
d) The medical term for period pains.

Answer: d)

CLEANSING SCIENTIFIC THOUGHT

Some researchers in America think that women have periods to spring-clean the uterus. It may surprise you to learn that every millilitre of fluid in a healthy woman's vagina contains millions of bacteria. These germs are kept out of the uterus by an acidic mucus that guards the cervix (neck of the womb). But the mucus breaks down to let sperm through. The germs grab their chance to travel up into the womb with the sperm. So a period flushes them back out again, keeping the uterus clean and healthy.

THE NOT-SO-SECRET

It's a good idea for a girl to keep a record of her menstrual cycle. It will help you to predict when your period will start.

DAY 1

FSH (Follicle Stimulating Hormone, if you recall) reaches an ovary in the womb. It has travelled in the bloodstream from the pituitary gland in the brain. Once it has arrived, it sets about the business of maturing one of the many thousands of eggs or ovum stored there.

The ovum begins to mature in a tiny sac called a 'follicle'.

The follicle starts to move towards the surface of the ovary.

DAY 5

The follicle produces the female hormone oestrogen. This sends a message to the the uterus, telling it to get ready to receive the egg in case it is fertilized.

The uterus starts to get ready for a possible pregnancy by thickening the lining of its wall with blood that will nourish the egg. At this time the lining is about 1 mm thick.

Meanwhile, the ovum is still maturing and gradually getting nearer to the surface of the ovary.

DIARY OF A PERIOD

DAY 14

The ovum is now mature. The pituitary gland stops producing FSH and begins to produce LH. This causes the ovum to burst out of the follicle and leave the ovary. This is called ovulation.

Some girls feel a slight pain at ovulation. Some may also notice that they have jelly-like white or yellow vaginal discharge.

The follicle from which the ovum has sprung starts to produce another female hormone, progesterone. This makes the lining of the uterus soft and spongy, so that the ovum can cling to it if it is fertilized.

Meanwhile, the ovum travels along the Fallopian tube towards the uterus.

DAY 21

The ovum arrives in the uterus. The lining is now about 5 mm thick. If the ovum has been fertilized, it embeds itself into the wall of the uterus and begins to develop into a baby.

If it is unfertilized, a series of things occur. The levels of oestrogen and progesterone fall. The ovum starts to disintegrate. The lining of the uterus begins to break up and come away from the walls. This causes some blood to escape. The blood, cells and some liquid from the womb flow from the body. The pituitary gland receives the message that there is no pregnancy and begins the cycle again.

HOW & WHY PERIODS HAPPEN

QUICK GUIDE

Every month, one of your ovaries releases an egg cell also known as an ovum. This can be fertilized by a male sperm (see page 39). The egg travels down the Fallopian tube to the womb. If the egg is fertilized it can develop into a baby. If not, it disintegrates.

MEANWHILE

While the egg has been developing and travelling, the lining of the uterus has been getting thicker. This happens in case the egg does get fertilized – it can then embed itself in the thick lining and grow. If the egg doesn't get fertilized, the lining isn't needed, so it breaks down. The cells, blood and other liquids that it is made of are then discharged from the body through the vagina. This is a period.

SLIGHTLY MORE SCIENTIFIC GUIDE

The menstrual cycle is controlled by those good old horror moans FSH and LH – remember them?

SYNCHRONIZED PERIODS

Often girls who live together (or spend a lot of time together) tend to have their periods at the same time! Although no one knows exactly why this happens, it may be to do with one girl's hormones passing signals to the next girl through sweat!

What's all this fertilization business?

When the egg cell has been released and begins its travels down the Fallopian tube, it can be fertilized by one of the sperm travelling up the Fallopian tube. This happens when a female has unprotected sexual intercourse with a male. (See page 91 for more detailed information about sexual intercourse.)

When a man puts his penis into a woman's vagina and orgasms, he will ejaculate semen. Semen is a liquid that contains millions of sperm. Sperm are the male sex cells.

When the sperm shoot out of the man's penis, they swim up the vagina, up through the womb and into the Fallopian tubes, hoping to meet an egg!

FERTILIZATION

Many millions of sperm are ejaculated into the female during sexual intercourse. Thousands of these sperm die in their attempt to reach the egg or ovum. When the survivors reach the ovum they all try to penetrate the egg together, but it takes only one sperm to complete fertilization of the egg.

It is also possible for sperm to enter the vagina even if a couple have not had full intercourse. If a man ejaculates near the opening of the vagina, it is still possible for the sperm to get into the vagina and swim up to the Fallopian tubes.

IN THE WOMB

If a sperm meets an egg and fertilizes it, the egg will continue its journey to the womb. Then it will embed itself into the spongy lining of the uterus and begin to develop into a baby. This stage is called implantation.

The developing baby is called an embryo. It begins to grow in the womb. After 8 weeks, it is called a foetus. By now it will be about 18 mm long and start to develop hands, face and all the major organs – heart, brain, lungs, liver and kidneys.

The foetus carries on growing for 9 months, attached to the wall of the womb by the placenta. All its nutrients are passed to it from its mother through the umbilical cord.

GIVING BIRTH

When the baby is ready to be born, the woman will go into labour. At this stage, the muscles in the uterus contract and push the baby towards the vagina. As the contractions come more quickly, the mother will help the birth by pushing down with her muscles, until eventually the baby is born, emerging from her body through the vagina. The length of labour varies greatly from one woman to another.

AGONY AUNT

Worried about your body? Don't know about periods?* Need something to do instead of your homework? Well, write to our very own agony aunt, Gladys Arkwright (aged 96).

Dear Auntie Gladys,
I am very worried! I am 45 and I've still not had my first period! Does this mean that I am pregnant, or just weird?
Love, Keith

Dear Keith,
You are a boy. Boys don't have periods.

Oi! Gladys, you old git,
Every month I suffer from the most incredible irritability and stress. So you'd better tell me how I can get rid of it, or else I'm round to yours with a large axe.
Liz (also known as 'Killer')

Dear Liz,
I think that you just might be suffering from PMT – what we experts call premenstrual tension. Some girls get this when they are about to start a period. Some women who get PMT find that taking vitamin B6 or evening primrose oil helps a little. It might also be a good wheeze to avoid coffee and fizzy drinks, and to try cutting down on sugar and fatty foods. Drinking even a little alcohol before a period can give you a really bad hangover. You should also take as much rest as you can, and not expect too much from yourself on the days leading up to your period.
PS Just thought I'd mention that I've got two rather big Rottweilers who are trained to attack anyone they see with large axes.
PPS You can read all about PMT on page 44.

* Then read the last few
  pages, QUICKTIME!

41

SANITARY PROTECTION

When you have a period, you will need to do something to stop the blood going everywhere. You have a choice. You can use sanitary towels or tampons. Keep a note of when your period is due, and keep a towel or tampon about your person. It's a good idea to wear panty liners when you're coming up to that dreaded time of the month. Suddenly finding your skirt or jeans soaked with blood can be bloody embarrassing!

Sanitary towels, also known as sanitary pads, are used to line the inside of your pants and are attached to a sanitary belt to keep them in place. Or you can buy press-on towels that have a sticky back that you stick inside your pants.

Sanitary towels are available in different sizes and thicknessess. Find the sort that are best for you by experimenting.

PLACES NOT TO PUT A TAMPON
- **Up nose**
- **In ear**
- **In mouth**
- **Up bottom**

Wear dark coloured clothes when having a period – just in case you forget to change the pad before it leaks.

TAMPONS

Tampons fit inside the vagina. They are made from tightly rolled cotton wool with a string attached to one end. Some come inside a cardboard tube that pushes the tampon into place. Others you insert with your fingers. Like sanitary towels, tampons come in various sizes and absorbencies. Inside the packet you will find instructions telling you how to insert a sanitary tampon. Once it's in position inside the vagina, you should not be able to feel it.

You can have a bath and go swimming with a tampon still in place. You'd get very soggy and messy if you tried to do this with a sanitary towel!

ALL CHANGE

PADS:

It is important to change sanitary pads regularly. This is because bacteria can make the pad smelly if you leave it on too long. A wet pad may also make you sore and uncomfortable.

● Change your pad every couple of hours if your bleeding is heavy.

● If bleeding is light, you may need to change it only two or three times a day. Judge for yourself.

TAMPONS:

It's not as easy to tell when a tampon needs changing – aim to do it before the string gets stained with blood! If you start by changing every couple of hours, you'll soon be able to gauge your flow. It's a good idea to put a fresh tampon in when you go to bed, and again when you get up in the morning. Some girls like to wear a panty liner for extra protection with a tampon – especially if they are doing something energetic.

What should I do with soiled towels and tampons?

Flush them down the loo only as a last resort. This is because sewage works have trouble processing tampons, and pads with plastic backs are even more of a problem. Towels can also easily block toilets! To stop sanitary bits and pieces ending up on the nation's beaches, you need to dispose of them properly. At home you can wrap them in a bag and put them in the bin. When you're out, you'll find that most Ladies toilets have a special bin for used tampons and pads. You can always carry a small plastic bag in your pocket for emergencies.

Toxic Shock Syndrome

Premenstral Tension

(TSS)

This is a very rare condition that can affect males and females. It happens when fast-growing bacteria enter the bloodstream. About 50 per cent of people who get Toxic Shock Syndrome are women who use certain types of very absorbent tampons. They get TSS when bacteria grow on the tampon. This is why it is essential to remember to change your tampon regularly.

Although TSS can cause death, we want to stress that it is extremely rare, so don't let it put you off using tampons.

What are the symptoms?

Signs of Toxic Shock Syndrome are high fever, vomiting and diarrhoea. You might have a rash and develop headaches as well as having aching muscles. If you have these symptoms, remove your tampon straight away and call a doctor.

(PMT OR PMS)

Premenstrual tension (PMT), also known as premenstrual syndrome (PMS), affects many women. As we have seen, the horror moans are extremely active in a girl's body just before she has her period, and this can make her moody, tense, depressed, irritable and unpredictable. It is caused by the falling levels of oestrogen and progesterone.

PMT can be a real problem, because it makes women argue, get weepy and depressed, and feel violent and out of control.

It is important to realize what's happening and to be considerate towards anyone suffering from PMT.

Reducing your intake of coffee and sugar, and avoiding alcohol will help. Also eating a balanced diet and getting plenty of rest is important. Remember, as awful as it seems at the time, it should last only a few days.

Do not confuse PMT with GMT, GMTV, RSVP, or PTO.

So why doesn't PMT happen to boys?

It's basically because boys don't have a hormone cycle, with horror moans switching on and off and causing all sorts of havoc. The male sex hormone level remains more or less the same every day while female hormones change all the time.

INTERESTING POINT

If you were in North America and your teacher told you that you had forgotten your period, it would mean that you'd made a punctuation mistake. A period is what Americans call a full stop!

MORE HORMONE HORRORS

Because hormones are carried through the blood and visit all parts of the body, it goes without saying that they create trouble everywhere. Other horror-moan effects that can wallop you just before or during a period are:

- **Sore, swollen breasts**
- **Headaches**
- **Spots**
- **Greasy skin and hair**
- **Swelling of the stomach, wrists, fingers, ankles and legs (called water retention)**
- **Tiredness and dizziness**
- **Clumsiness**

Great hey? NOT!

The good thing to remember is that you shouldn't get all of these lovely symptoms at the same time (unless you're very, very unlucky, that is)!

Daft Dick Says...

WHEN YOU'RE HAVING A PERIOD YOU SHOULDN'T

- **HAVE A BATH OR WASH YOUR HAIR**
  Wrong! This is an old superstition and is totally crackers! It is important to be clean ALL the time.

- **SWIM**
  There's no reason why you should give up swimming. A tampon will not show when you're in your swimsuit, and nor will it soak up water from the pool.

- **DO ANY EXERCISE**
  Garbage! In fact, exercise can help relieve period pain by stretching the stomach muscles.

PERIOD EXCUSE

Periods do have their advantages at home and at school. They are great for getting out of doing boring lessons or helping with tedious chores!

Try these:

SCENE: AT HOME

Mum has just asked you to help out with some housework.

You say: *"I'd like to, Mum, but I'm not feeling well, because it's that time of month. So please don't shout at me or make me do any washing-up/cleaning/hoovering/shopping/dusting etc., or else I'll probably get terribly emotional and burst out crying and then you'll feel guilty."*

WARNING!!!

This excuse is best used on your mother – your dad will probably say one of the following:

"What's that got to do with anything?"

"I'm sure it doesn't hurt that much."

"God, you're getting just like your mother!"

EXCUSES, EXCUSES

If you are stuck in a boring lesson with a male teacher, you could try the following:

Either:

a) **Put your hand up and wait for the teacher to ask you to speak. This is VERY effective.**

Or:

b) **Go up to his desk, quietly clutching your stomach.**

PUPIL: *"Can I go and lie down in the medical room, sir?"*
  (Make sure that this line is given in a soft and pained voice. Try it with eyes cast down to the ground as if a little embarrassed.)

MALE TEACHER: *"Why?"*
  (This line will usually come snapping back like a slap in the face! If you've tried the sitting-at-your-desk approach the whole class will be looking round at this point. Take full advantage of all the attention!)

PUPIL: *"Girl problems."*
  (Look embarrassed and deliver the line in a downbeat mumble. Don't be aggressive. The soft approach works like a dream!)

MALE TEACHER: *"Oh, erm, er...."*
  (Brilliant! He's now totally gutted and his original snapping makes him look like a cretin. If you have employed the next-to-the-desk technique, he will look around the room hoping that others haven't heard.)

PUPIL: *"Please, sir?"*

> *(Make your voice really plaintive, and get in quickly with this line while he is in a state of confusion – just to make him feel even more guilty!)*

TEACHER: *"Yes, yes, off you go. Quickly, now!"*

> *(He will practically throw you out of the room and hope that if all the class witnessed this, they will think he's a model of kindness, caring and understanding.)*

The great thing about this is that you haven't actually said what the problem is! 'Girl problems' could be anything from period pains to the fact that your favourite pop group have split up!

In a PE lesson you might try the following:

PUPIL: *"I can't do sport, I'm on."*

The problem is that most sports teachers won't take this as an excuse, even if you've brought a note from your mum or taken a doctor to school with you to vouch for your trustworthiness!

Your teacher will probably tell you not to be so pathetic and to get on with it, because when the body is active it releases endorphins. These are natural painkillers. It means that doing sport will be good for you! There's just no way out if your PE teacher belongs to this monster race.

TIPS

- *Don't use these excuses more than once a month! (You can, of course, use them at different times of the month with different teachers, and they are more effective with male teachers.)*
- *Don't try these excuses if you are a boy.*

Chapter 7

Hygiene

HYGIENE – YES, WE MEAN BOYS AS WELL AS GIRLS!

Why is it so important to keep clean?

1 If you don't, you'll start to smell disgusting.

2 No one will want to sit next to you.

3 Bacteria just love unclean bodies. (You could get ill.)

4 Washing has been known to get rid of dead skin, dirt, bacteria, sweat, grease and felt-tip pen marks.

5 If you smell good, you'll be more attractive to others than if you smell like the back end of a pig (unless you're also a pig, of course).

QUICK QUIZ

What is BO?

a) A pop group.
b) An award from the Queen.
c) A new exam.
d) Body odour.
e) An abbreviation of "bugger off!"

Answer: d)

SWEAT IT OUT

Even your sweat glands want to join in the action when you reach puberty. They get themselves into the spirit by producing more sweat, which then gushes out of the pores in your skin.

Sweat is great. It helps you to get rid of body waste and helps to control body temperature. However, the bad news is that sweat can develop a particularly choking smell when it dries and bacteria start to feed on it. It can also cause serious embarrassment in a public place if you happen to look under your armpits and discover massive wet circles on your shirt or blouse. You can avoid getting smelly by using a deodorant or anti-perspirant.

What's the difference between deodorants and anti-perspirants?

Deodorants slow down the growth of bacteria and cover body odour with perfume. Anti-perspirants close up some of the pores, so sweat can't get out. They may also contain a deodorant.

There are sweat glands around your genitals as well as under your arms, so it is important to wash your privates every day with warm water and MILD soap to keep them clean and healthy.

Bacteria absolutely love to feed on scrummy vaginal fluids, urine, smegma, semen and menstrual blood. So, even more reasons to keep those privates fresh as daisies!

Girls should remember to wash backwards from the vulva towards the anus. This is to avoid transferring bacteria from the anus into the vaginal opening which could cause infection.

Boys with foreskins should remember to pull back the foreskin and wash under it carefully.

WARNING!!

Don't put underarm deodorants and anti-perspirants anywhere near your genitals, and don't be tempted to use so-called vaginal deodorants. They may well cause you to itch like crazy and could even lead to an infection.

Hair

Do you have lank, greasy hair?
When you shake your head
do you produce a blizzard
of dandruff?
Yes?
Well, don't worry, because
now you too can have a head
of trouble-free hair!
Just wash it with
BARLOW & SKIDMORE'S
INSTANT HAIR REMOVER!
Just wash it once and see
your hair drop out.
You'll never again be worried
by dandruff or suffer from
greasy uncontrollable hair.

Because you
won't have
any hair
to worry
about!

Your hair can be your
crowning glory if you look
after it. Do you want to
spend the rest of your life
wearing funny hats, or
would you rather let it
all hang out?

You should wash your hair on a regular basis to get rid of dead skin, dirt, sebum (grease) and sweat. If you notice white flakes in your hair, this is dandruff. The tiny flakes are bits of dead skin falling off your scalp. No need to panic! Get rid of dandruff with a medicated shampoo.

ROYAL YUK

On a royal visit to Australia in 1983, Princess Diana (when she was still married to Charles) went walkabout into the waiting crowds. Meeting one small loveable Aussie kid, she patted him on the head and tousled his hair, asking why he wasn't at school. The kid replied: "I've been sent home, 'cos I've got head lice!"

51

Teeth

Keep 'em clean and you'll keep 'em longer! Tooth decay is caused by sugar-loving bacteria that settle on your teeth and harden into plaque. This is acidic and eats into the tooth. If the resulting hole isn't filled, you'll probably develop toothache and eventually lose the tooth.

WAYS TO LOSE YOUR TEETH

- Bend a poker in your teeth
- Pick a fight with a gang
- Run into a brick wall
- Don't brush your teeth

TEETH top tips

Brush your teeth two or three times a day, preferably after meals. Brush up and down, not across.
Visit a dentist regularly – get your teeth checked out every six months.
Eat fewer sugary foods and sweets.
Use a fluoride toothpaste.
Don't use anybody else's toothbrush – you could pick up an infection.
Floss your teeth regularly.

GET RID OF YOUR SPOTS – FOR EVER!

Ever been embarrassed by a humungous ugly spot erupting like a volcano just before a special night out? Can't pull the girls or the boys because of your zitty appearance?
Do you spend a fortune on spot cream?
Yes? Well, this is for you!!

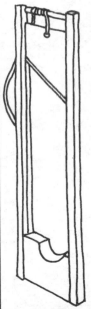

We can help you get rid of your spots – for ever.
No greasy lotions! No messy creams!
No more hours of squeezing those blackheads!
You can get rid of your spotty face in one fell swoop with our patent machine:

a guillotine!

For best results, place your head over the wood support (rest your head on a padded cushion to make you feel especially comfy). Pull the cord and listen to the razor-sharp blade as it plummets towards your neck. A split second later, and voilà! No more troublesome spots! This fabulous machine can also help with weight loss! If, after using the guillotine, you are not 100 per cent satisfied, simply return the guillotine to us and we will refund your money in the twinkle of a blade!

Problem Skin

One of the major problems of puberty for many people is spots. They have the annoying habit of appearing right at the wrong moment in embarrassing places like the end of your nose. You might just as well erect a neon sign on your face saying 'SPOT!'

SPOT THE DIFFERENCE

Blackheads happen when sebum builds up at the opening of a sebaceous gland. Whiteheads happen when sebum builds up below the surface of the skin. Whiteheads are also caused by bacteria.

Foolproof methods of hiding zits

- Paper bag placed over head
- Bucket over head
- Join up your spots with a pen and claim you are a living example of dot-to-dot artwork
- Only go out at night in thick fog

Dr Ivel Says...

During puberty your sebaceous glands produce bucketfuls of sebum, an oily substance that stops your skin and hair from drying out too much. It also keeps it waterproof. However, too much sebum can build up and cause blackheads and whiteheads. Infected spots at their worst are called acne and can affect your face, back and shoulders.

SO HOW CAN I GET RID OF ACNE?

- *Don't ever pick or squeeze acne – it will make the infection spread, and may leave permanent scars.*
- *Keep your skin clean – gently! Use pH-balanced soaps or detergent cleaners that don't contain drying and harmful chemicals.*
- *Cleanse your skin from the inside. Give up sweets, sugary soft drinks and fatty foods such as nuts and fry-ups. Eat more fresh fruit and raw vegetables. Drink fresh fruit and veg juices and lots of water.*
- *Boost your vitamin intake. A, B group and C and E vitamins are especially good for your skin.*
- *If your acne is worrying go and see your doctor. If necessary, he will be able to prescribe medical creams or other treatments to help the condition. If your case is very severe, he may refer you to a dermatologist – a doctor that specializes in skin care.*

HOW CAN I GET RID OF BLACKHEADS?

The best way to get rid of blackheads is to use an exfoliating scrub (don't use it on acne). A scrub is a paste with a gritty texture. The grit might be tiny bits of oatmeal, or even powdered dried beans. Wash your face, then rub the paste into the skin around your nose and chin, where blackheads like to lurk. Wash the paste off with cold water. You'll probably need to use this treatment once a week for clean, healthy-looking skin.

Some people enjoy squeezing blackheads. If you absolutely must, here's how to do it without scarring yourself for life!

- Make sure your hands are clean.
- Warm your face with a hot towel or, even better, over a bowl of steaming water. This opens up the pores.
- With your fingers inside a paper handkerchief, squeeze the blackhead – do this gently to avoid bruising. Don't dig into the skin with your nails.
- Bathe the skin with cold water, or witch-hazel on cotton wool.

EVERYDAY SKIN CARE

Wash your face frequently with unperfumed, antiseptic soap or an anti-bacterial face wash. Use warm water to soften the skin and open the pores, then give a final rinse with fresh cold water to close them again. Pat your face dry gently with a clean towel.

Keep a towel for your own personal use. This stops other people's bacteria ending up on your face!

SPOT THE FACT: 1
There are more sebaceous glands on your back and face. That's why you get more pimples there.

SPOT THE FACT: 2
Experts think the male sex hormone, testosterone, is largely to blame for producing sebum. That's why boys usually get more pimples than girls.

SUN SPOT
It is thought that the ultraviolet (UV) rays in sunlight can act as an antiseptic and dry out spots. (But too much sun can give you skin cancer!)

MORE SPOT TRUTHS
There's another reason why you might get spots. You are covered in millions of bacteria. And the YUKKO fact is that these teeny microscopic creatures feed on you! That's right – you're lunch!

Human Body Restaurant

Menu

Sweat
Skin oil
Dead skin

This is a really delicious à la carte, Egon Ronay-approved, nouvelle cuisine, dish-of-the-day menu for the millions of bacteria that live on your skin. They particularly enjoy nibbling away in pores blocked with scrummy sebum. And this leads to a big fight in your body.

Welcome to the Spotweight Championship of the body. It's the body versus those sneaky little bacteria! The body doesn't look in very good shape. It's going through that tricky age of puberty, so there's a lot of sebum swilling about in there. I also hear rumours that the body hasn't been in training lately. It looks as though the diet of chips, burgers and chocolate hasn't helped. The skin has a tell-tale pale and greasy sheen, suggesting infrequent contact with soap and water.

DING DING, ROUND ONE!

The bacteria are off to a good start, getting into the body through a blocked sebaceous gland while the white cells weren't looking. It's their job to fight infection, but the white cells haven't even made an effort! And now there's some swelling under the body's skin. The referee is having a look....

DING DING!

Saved by the bell! Well, unless the body can come up with some white cells, it looks as though it's going to be all over very quickly.

DING DING, ROUND TWO!

Ah! Now the white cells are coming back. They've been carried into the ring by the blood. They've seen the bacteria – and here they go! A left, a right, another left! The bacteria are struggling now. I can see real swelling under the skin. There are great lumps forming, swollen by the fight between blood and bacteria!

DING DING!

What a fight! The white cells and bacteria are slugging it out and there's so much pus being formed these great swellings could burst any minute!

DING DING, ROUND THREE!

The white cells are now really on top. The bacteria are losing ground, being literally eaten up by the cells. The swelling is going down. The redness in the skin seems to be reducing. And the referee's stopped the fight! The bacteria are beaten! The white cells have saved the day and the skin can return to normal. Phew! I hope you can join us for the next Spotweight fight.

Even Lady Macbeth couldn't resist picking at her spots.

"Out, out, damned spot!"

SPOT ON!

A fun idea is to try for a bull's-eye when you're busting your zits. This is best done alone or with a friend who has a similarly warped sense of fun. Draw a target directly on the mirror with your mum's or your sister's best lipstick. Sit comfortably, take aim and squeeze those pimples! After a good session don't forget to wipe the mirror, or you could get into major trouble!

PUBES AND PIMPLES COMPETITION

Spot the spot! Win a million!*

We have removed the spot from the face. Using your skill and judgement, mark an 'X' where you think the spot is. You can mark up to 10 crosses.

COST

1 cross	£3,000
2 crosses	£5,000
5 crosses	£10,000
10 crosses	£15,000

Send your entry and the money to this address:
Barlow & Skidmore,
Secret Bank Account,
Geneva,
Switzerland

We will announce the winner in 10 year's time (maybe)

* (A million spots)

Chapter 8

Diet & Exercise

This is what a typical teenager would like to eat all the time.

This is what an unhealthy diet looks like.

All food gives you energy. This energy is measured in calories. During puberty a boy needs about 3,000 calories a day and a girl 2,100. The calories you eat are burnt off during the day. Exercise can get rid of more calories. People put on weight because they eat more calories than they burn off. Excess calories are stored under the skin as fat.

As you grow, it's important that you eat a varied and healthy diet, with plenty of vegetables and fruit, and not too much sugar and fat. Here is what you need for a balanced and healthy diet.

PROTEIN

You need protein to help the body grow and repair itself. You'll get protein in lean meat, eggs, fish, milk, cheese, nuts and pulses (beans and peas). If you are a vegetarian, it is especially important that you get enough protein from other sources, such as beans and lentils and dairy products. It might be worth considering taking a supplement.

CARBOHYDRATES

Carbohydrates act like fuel and provide the body with energy. Carbohydrates are found in starchy and sugary foods, but those in sugary foods are called 'empty carbohydrates' because they contain no nourishment. So, while you need to avoid sweets, fizzy drinks, chocolate, cakes, and biscuits (because the sugar in them will give you spots and bad teeth), you should eat plenty of starchy foods like wholemeal bread, potatoes, rice and pasta.

FATS

There are also good and bad fats. The fats to avoid are heavy fats (also called 'saturated' fats), like cream and the fat on meat (cut it off). This sort of fat can cause heart trouble in later life. Too much butter or cheese isn't good for you either, for the same reason. One fat that's really good for your health (and especially good for your heart) is olive oil. It's a monounsaturated fat. See if there's some in your kitchen. It's delicious on salads and pasta, and you can cook with it too. Fish oils are also a good source of this type of fat.

VITAMINS & MINERALS

Vitamins and minerals occur naturally in most foods. We need small amounts of these on a regular basis to keep healthy. Here are some of the key vitamins and minerals, the foods you can find them in, and what they do for your body.

Vitamins

Vitamin A
liver, fish oil, dairy products,
fruit and vegetables
for healthy eyes, skin and tissue

Vitamin B
meat, Marmite, dairy products,
wholemeal bread, oily fish, nuts,
green leafy vegetables, for the brain,
nerves and red blood cells

Vitamin C
citrus fruits, blackcurrants, green
vegetables (especially parsley
and watercress)
for immunity against disease

Vitamin D
oily fish, dairy products, eggs
(also from the sun)
for bone growth

Vitamin E
nuts, wheatgerm, eggs, green leafy
vegetables, wholemeal bread
for fighting disease

Vitamin K
green vegetables (especially sprouts,
broccoli and spinach)
for healing wounds

Minerals

Calcium
milk and cheese
for strong bones and teeth

Sodium
salt
for muscles and nerves

Zinc
seafood, pork, dairy products,
green vegetables for
growth and development

Phosphorus
cheese, canned fish, eggs, yoghurt
for healthy bones and
strong teeth

Potassium
apples, bananas, carrots, broccoli
for cells and nervous tissue

Magnesium
soya beans, nuts, yeast
for energy, nerves and muscles

FIBRE

Fibre is very important in the diet, because it helps with digestion and the elimination of waste. It prevents constipation and will protect you against diseases of the stomach and bowel (such as cancer) later in life.

Another word for fibre is 'roughage'. It's generally the bulky, stringy bits (the cell walls) found in fruit, cereals and vegetables. Other fibre-rich foods are pulses, nuts, rice, pasta, muesli, bran and wholemeal bread. When you eat these foods, the vitamins and minerals in them are absorbed into your bloodstream, and the fibre is left behind in the gut. It bulks up, collecting other debris in your intestines, and is passed as faeces.

Anorexia nervosa

This is a serious illness more common in girls than boys. Anyone suffering from anorexia nervosa has very low self-esteem, believing that they're too fat when they aren't. This leads to an obsession with slimming to the point of hardly eating at all. People suffering from anorexia do not see themselves as they really are – they look in the mirror and see a fat person, even though they are usually painfully thin. Anorexic girls can get dangerously thin. They often get ill and their periods stop. Anyone with anorexia needs professional help, including counselling to help with self-esteem. Appetite and good health will gradually return.

Bulimia

Bulimia is another serious eating disorder. Girls are more likely to suffer from it than boys. A girl with bulimia is probably very depressed and feels unloved. She secretly stuffs herself with food in an effort to give herself comfort, then feels horrified and guilty at the amount she's eaten. She makes herself sick. Bulimia can be more difficult to diagnose than anorexia, because the patient may eat normally in public and often doesn't become very thin. Bulimia patients need help from a counsellor to make them feel better about themselves so that they can break the pattern of bingeing and vomiting. In time they will return to a healthy and guilt-free enjoyment of food.

EXERCISE

It's important to exercise during puberty in order to help your body develop. A fit person is more likely to avoid illness in later life.

BUT! For some people exercise can be as much fun as pulling out your fingernails.

Reasons:

- Hating team games you are forced to play at school by bullying PE teachers

- Being embarrassed at how your body looks

- Feeling that you are 'bad' at a sport and fearing criticism

HEY! It doesn't have to be like that! Apart from the team games you play at school, there are dozens of other ways of getting exercise.

- **Horseriding**
- **Swimming**
- **Cycling**
- **Aerobics**
- **Weight training**
- **Dancing**
- **Walking**
- **Tennis**
- **Jogging**

Any form of exercise is better than none at all. Choose one that you enjoy and give it a go. Stick at it for a little while and get into a routine. It could grow on you! Exercise is also a great way of meeting people and developing friendships.

WHAT EXERCISE DOES FOR YOU

- *Develops muscles, making them stronger and more efficient* • *Keeps joints supple*•
- *Improves circulation* • *Improves reflexes and coordination* • *Improves stamina* • *Helps you relax* • *Keeps you slim* • *Boosts energy levels and gives you zest for life*

SLEEP

Do you fancy telling your parents that you have to lie in bed all day because of a medical reason?

Try this! Because you are growing, you are using up loads of energy, so you need more rest and sleep. Ten to fourteen-year-olds need an average of ten hours sleep a night. Fourteen to eighteen-year-olds need around nine hours. While you are asleep, your body is recovering the energy you lost through growing!

WARNING!!!

Some parents will take the opportunity of waking you from your delicious morning slumber to get their own back – for when you used to wake them up as a little kid! We're sure they'll take great delight in prodding you into early-morning action!

Chapter 9

Emotions & other Pressures

Calling all Jekyll and Hydes – you're only normal!

It's not only your body that makes major changes during puberty, it is also your personality. This may lead to some problems with your nearest and dearest, who are going to have to put up with your changeable nature.

WHO ME? If you ever hear a grown-up describing someone as a 'typical adolescent', they probably mean one of the following:

- *What a ******!*
- *What an inconsiderate ******!!*
- *What a bad-mannered ******!*
- *What a horrible ******!*
- *What an immature ******!*
- *What an ungrateful ******!*
- *What a selfish ******!*

*(We'll leave you to fill in what ******! is)*

They are more than likely referring to the fact that they think the typical adolescent is behaving in a way they consider to be negative. If not downright antisocial and psychotic.

So why are teenagers and adolescents seen as such uncontrollable monsters?

As you hit puberty you get physically bigger and begin to feel more independent, after all, you're nearly an adult.

So, you'll want to make more decisions about your own life, what you wear, what kind of hairstyle you have, what friends you see, what time you go to bed etc. The problem is that your parents aren't used to you making your own decisions about your life – they're used to making them for you.

As you grow more and more independent and want more freedom, other people will become more important to you than your parents (close friends, boyfriends, girlfriends). This can be difficult for parents to accept.

There is also the problem of the 'generation gap'. Your parents were brought up with different values and rules. They may find it difficult to accept your ideas and beliefs – in the same way that you may find it difficult to accept theirs. All of this can lead to major arguments.

Guaranteed parental sayings

"You're not going out dressed like that!"

"Where are you going?"

"You treat this house like a hotel."

"What on earth is that noise you're playing?"

"You could give some help around the house."

"You're not going out until you've done your homework."

"Don't talk to me like that."

"I want you in by nine o'clock!"

"You're not going out with him/her!"

"Are you still on that phone?"

"It's my house and you do what I say!"

All of these can lead to arguments. How? Easily!

> Parent: "You're not going dressed like that!"
> You: "Why not?"
> (Note: This is a reasonable request, but one that will lead to trouble, because there isn't usually a reasonable answer.)
> Parent: "Because you're not!"
> You: "Why not?"
> Parent: (Inevitably) "Because I say so!"

Unfortunately, "Because I say so" doesn't hold water with you any more – you want reasons and many parents aren't used to giving you reasons. Therefore World War III is possible.

BE MATURE

However, try to remember that your parents are human (though that may sometimes be difficult to believe!) – and remember this golden rule – for every action there is a reaction. Therefore, if you act well towards your parents, they'll react well towards you. If you act badly, you'll probably get a bad reaction back. So negotiate with your parents. For instance, you could try to strike a bargain. "If I do all the dusting, hoovering and washing-up for the next 5 years, will you let me go to my friend's party on Saturday?"

If you act maturely and responsibly, your parents will treat you in a more adult way. And they ought to understand how you feel if you talk to them, because they were young once.

FOUL FACTS

Some people do not come from a happy family background – their parents may be splitting up, or someone in the house may be suffering violence or abuse. If this is happening to you, try to find adult support outside the family. Choose someone you trust and can talk to easily. This might be another relative, an older friend, your doctor or a teacher.

I HATE MYSELF!

Another person you may get upset with is yourself!

With all those horror moans causing havoc with your body, it's no wonder that you feel moody, grumpy and emotional. Some teenagers worry about everything, including their appearance, their friends, and even their private thoughts. This is quite normal, and you won't always feel so bad. Remember, people can't see that swampy field of self-doubt inside you or read your thoughts. They probably think far more highly of you than you realize.

Moods can be measured on the PUBERTY UNPLUGGED SWINGOMETER.

| Everyone loves me, I'm brilliant | | Everyone hates me, I'm terrible |

Your mood will usually be somewhere on this scale!
(Mind you, so will everyone else's!)

FRIENDS

Puberty can be a great time for making friends. However, it is also guaranteed that you will fall out with some people because of the changes you are going through. Although this can be pretty horrible and sad, you will have to accept that you can't always get on with everybody. Sometimes you can outgrow a friendship. It's a fact of life, and part of growing up!

Two particular problems that affect the teenage social scene are bullying and peer-group pressure. If you're suffering from either of these, it's good to tell an adult you can trust, because you're going to need help from outside the group.

BULLIES

A bully is someone who picks on you and pushes you around. Bullies tend to be people who don't like themselves and have to exercise power over others to make themselves feel more important. Bullying can also happen on a larger scale between groups or gangs. Either way, it causes all sorts of distress and emotional upset.

If you feel you are being bullied, TELL SOMEONE.

Some people feel bad about doing this as the bullies might have threatened them or they feel that people shouldn't 'grass' on others. Forget all this. It is VITAL that you let someone else know what's going on.

If you are a bully, ask yourself what you get out of it. Why do you do it? Does it make you feel big? More powerful?

Do you think that people will like you more if you can show how tough you are? In fact, being a bully shows that you have a real problem with your own self-worth. You don't think well of yourself unless you're hurting someone else. If you start liking yourself more, you'll realize that you are equal to other people. Then you won't have to squash them to make yourself heard. And just think of the pleasure you'll get out of being liked and being one of the crowd.

Peer-group pressure

If you feel you have to do something because your friends expect you to, or tell you to, this is peer-group pressure. You want to be liked and you think the best way of being accepted by others is to do what they are doing or say you should do.

It's important that you do only what YOU want to do and what you feel is right. Don't let others persuade you to do anything you don't want to. In many cases, it is peer-group pressure that makes teenagers start to drink alcohol, smoke cigarettes, have sex before they want to or take illegal drugs.

It's inevitable that at some time during your teenage years, you'll come into contact with drugs. Some drugs are more dangerous than others. Do you know which are the drugs you're most at risk from? We think you're in for a big surprise. The drugs most likely to do serious damage to your health are alcohol and tobacco.

These are the drugs it's most difficult to say no to, because they're legal, readily available and widely used, even by people you look up to. You must be able to think of plenty of adults you like and admire who drink and smoke. So why should you say no? Here are two good reasons for saying no:

- *Tobacco is the world's biggest killer drug.*
- *Alcohol is the world's second biggest killer drug.*

71

We'd like you to read on and make up your own mind about smoking and drinking. But whatever you do, don't forget those two good reasons for not doing it. They're absolutely true, and you can probably surprise your friends with them – and your parents!

Tobacco

Every year around the world, a million people die of smoking-related diseases. Smoking can cause lung cancer, bronchitis, ulcers, heart disease and circulatory disorders.

Cigarette smoke contains 4,000 different chemicals, including two incredibly dangerous ones: nicotine and tar. Nicotine is one of the deadliest drugs in the world. In its purest concentrated form a single drop can kill a human being. In cigarettes, it makes the heart beat faster, narrows the blood vessels and affects the nervous system, causing a short-term high and a long-term depression. Tar blocks up your air passages and destroys the lining of your lungs. This makes breathing difficult and painful and causes respiratory diseases such as emphysema, asthma and lung cancer, all of which can kill.

The more you smoke, the more addicted to smoking you will become. The simple solution to this problem is don't start smoking in the first place.

Apart from the devastating consequences that smoking can have on your lungs, the habit also has other nasty side effects. Nicotine makes your hair dull and lifeless and brings your skin out in a sallow complexion which is more prone to spots. It can even cause your face to age prematurely. To make things worse, cigarette smoke makes you smell stale and unpleasant, like an old ashtray!

Alcohol

Like nicotine, alcohol is an addictive drug that can damage your body. It can eventually cause ulcers, liver disease, brain cell destruction, and damage to kidneys and blood vessels. (It also makes you fat.) It contains a lot of calories and hardly any nutrients.

Alcohol is present in drinks such as beer, cider, wine and spirits (e.g. vodka, rum, whisky). Manufacturers have also recently started producing fizzy drinks like lemonade that have an alcoholic content. Alcohol is a depressant. Although you may feel lively after a couple of drinks, if you carry on drinking your reactions will slow down, your thoughts become muddled, your inhibitions vanish and you can throw up or black out.

It is important never, never to drive with alcohol inside you, and never to encourage any of your friends to drink and drive.

Drink driving can kill.

On the morning after too much to drink you will probably suffer memory loss. You will also feel very ill and have a bad sick headache and churning stomach. This is a hangover, caused by dehydration and poisons in your brain.

At some point during your teenage years, you're almost bound to try something stupid with alcohol. Most people do, including parents. However, since drinking can also be very enjoyable, it's worth teaching yourself how to drink without getting drunk or making yourself ill. Here are a few tips:

Don't drink on an empty stomach.

Don't mix different types of drink, for example, wine, beer and spirits.

This is particularly useful to remember when you're at a party where you may get drinks thrust at you from all sides.

73

DRINK SAFETY GUIDE

- If you're drinking wine, try spritzer – this is white wine mixed half and half with soda and ice.

- If you're eating out, order a bottle of water as well as an alcoholic drink. Drink as much water as you can to pace yourself and dilute the alcohol. It's quite all right to drink wine and water together in the same glass. Remember, wine adds a lot extra to the bill.

- If you're drinking beer, try a shandy – beer and lemonade mixed. Or try a special low-alcohol beer.

- Look on the bottle label to check the strength of what you're drinking. Spirits are the strongest drinks (around 40 or 60 per cent alcohol). Wine is generally 12 to 15 per cent. Strong beers and ciders are up to about 8 per cent, and ordinary beers and ciders 3 to 6 per cent.

- Never be afraid to order non-alcoholic drinks, either all the time or for the rest of the evening after a couple of beers or glasses of wine. Flavoured waters, herbal drinks, fruit and vegetable cocktails and mineral waters are delicious, good for your health and leave you with loads of energy and all your faculties intact!

- Learn to recognize when your body has had enough, and learn to say 'no' without embarrassment.

- Try to avoid situations where you're buying large rounds.

- Carry a condom in a situation where you think drinking may lead to sex.

- Don't mix alcohol with other drugs, especially opiates, tranquillisers and barbiturates.

- Never drink and drive.

Street Drugs

As with alcohol and tobacco, you should know the risks associated with any street drugs.

Amphetamines

Originally developed to treat depression, amphetamines can be snorted up the nose in powder form, taken by mouth as capsules, smoked or injected. Amphetamines keep the user wide awake for hours, after which there may be extreme tiredness and feelings of anxiety. Users may feel tired and depressed when off the drug.

Barbiturates

Originally used to treat anxiety and depression, these are usually found in the form of tablets or capsules. Barbiturates are sedatives and have a similar effect on the body to alcohol. Users may get hostile and aggressive, and are prone to accidents. There is a high risk of a fatal overdose. There are severe withdrawal symptoms.

Cannabis

The leaves of the cannabis plant are smoked or eaten. It can make users relaxed or anxious. It also affects concentration and lowers inhibitions.

Cocaine and crack

Derived from the coca shrub, cocaine is a white powder, and crack is a concentrated form which comes in lumps. Cocaine is sniffed up the nose, while crack is heated and the smoke inhaled. Can make the user anxious and depressed. Cocaine sniffing can damage the lining of the nose. Repeated use of cocaine or crack can cause paranoia. Crack is very strongly addictive.

Ecstasy

This comes as tablets or capsules. It is a popular dance drug. Users report increased energy and feelings of goodwill. Sometimes there can be nausea and loss of appetite. Non-stop dancing can lead to overheating and dehydration. Some users have fallen into a coma, and there have been deaths.

Heroin

Derived from the opium poppy, heroin is one of many 'opiates'. It is a strong sedative used for pain relief in the terminally ill. As a street drug, heroin is addictive, with severe withdrawal symptoms. In large doses it can cause coma or kill. It can be smoked or sniffed but is usually injected. There is increased risk from infection with HIV through sharing needles. Methadone is often prescribed as a treatment for heroin addiction.

LSD

This very unpredictable hallucinogen comes as tablets or impregnated paper squares. Causes sight and sound distortions. An LSD trip can be extremely frightening, with feelings of persecution and panic. Accidents often occur.

Mushrooms

Eaten raw or cooked, they induce mild hallucinations. Two types of wild 'magic' mushrooms are used, liberty cap and fly agaric. They can cause anxiety and vomiting. There is an increased danger of accidents. There is also a danger of eating the wrong type of mushroom and getting severe poisoning.

Nitrates

A golden liquid, nitrates or 'poppers' come in little bottles that are popped open and sniffed or breathed in through the mouth. The effect is an immediate rushing feeling. Some users claim poppers increase sexual pleasure. They also cause loss of balance, headaches and vomiting. Drinking instead of sniffing this drug can kill. Regular use may lead to skin problems around the nose and mouth. The drug increases the heart rate and pressure in the eyeball.

Solvents

Glue, lighter fuel, aerosols, petrol, nail varnish remover and other fluids in everyday use are sniffed or breathed in through the mouth. Some users report light-headedness, others nausea and sleepiness. There is an increased risk of accidents. In about 45 minutes the effects wear off and there maybe a hangover. Deaths have been reported.

Steroids

Steroids can be taken illegally in gyms to help body-building. They are taken as pills or injected. Users may be at risk from infected needles. Heavy use can lead to aggressive behaviour and physical damage as well as problems with fertility, hormones and growth.

Tranquillisers

These are prescribed as sedatives for a number of illnesses such as anxiety, depression and insomnia. The street drugs are taken as pills or injected. Users may be at risk from infected needles. Users easily become addicted and withdrawal symptoms are severe. At first these drugs just calm the nerves, but with repeated use they cause anxiety and memory loss. Can be fatal with alcohol.

DRUGS AND THE LAW

The law relating to drug use, and to possession, supply, cultivation and manufacture of drugs is extremely complicated. Sentences are stiff. Class A drugs include cocaine, crack, ecstasy, heroin, LSD and any Class B drug prepared for injection. Anyone in possession of these drugs can get up to 7 years, and a supplier can get life imprisonment. Class B drugs include cannabis, amphetamines, barbiturates. Anyone in possession can get 5 years; supplying can get 14 years. Class C drugs include tranquillisers. Anyone in possession can get 2 years; supplying can get 5 years.

WARNING!

Injecting any drug can carry the risk of infection with the AIDS virus HIV if equipment is shared.

Chapter 10

Sex

Why do we bother? Read on and find out!

When girls become teenagers they begin to discover the attractions of boys.

Sometime after girls have taken up their new interest, boys begin to wonder whether there's more to life than comics, Airfix kits, computer games and fantasy football.

Unfortunately, this often doesn't happen until *QUITE A LONG TIME LATER.*

This is tough on girls.

After all, what is the point of spending a fortune on make-up, clothes and deodorant and getting your friend to do your hair just right, only to stand for hours round a freezing football pitch fluttering your eyelashes at the object of your desire, when the love of his life is Eric Cantona and he only has eyes for the ball?

MAKE YOUR OWN GIRL KIT

Have a photograph taken of yourself and stick it on the front of a very large cardboard box. Have somebody saw your body into bits and number them. Get a friend to put the bits in the box along with instructions and some glue, and give it to the boy of your dreams. He can put you together and fall hopelessly in love with his creation. But, he'll probably fail to read the instructions properly and put the bits together in the wrong order!

Favourite female tactics for attracting the male

1. The GBH ploy

The Lady hits the Gentleman with her schoolbag and runs away giggling.

2. The go-between

A friend with a big mouth tells the Gentleman, on the Lady's behalf, "Oi! Ugly! My mate fancies you!"

3. The letter

The Lady writes a letter to the Gentleman during a Biology class. This is then snatched from her and passed around all the Ladies in the Year until it is confiscated by the Only Really Dishy Teacher on the Staff. The Lady wants to die of deep embarrassment as she imagines that the Really Dishy Teacher will be passing her burning words of red hot passion around the staffroom and all the other teachers will be having a good laugh at her expense. *She will be dead right.*

Favourite male tactics for attracting the female

1. The showing-off stratagem

The Gentleman performs a difficult feat (walking on his hands, riding his bicycle with no hands, climbing on to the school roof etc.). He must make sure the Lady is watching, but must be careful not to look at her at any time.

2. The "I'm dead 'ard, me" scam

The Gentleman will stand around with some tough mates talking in loud voices and guffawing noisily, especially while the Lady is looking. (Exactly why this is supposed to be attractive to the Lady is unclear.)

3. The indirect approach

The Gentleman causes a message to be sent to the Lady through so many intermediaries that if the Lady happens to reply, "I wouldn't go out with that creep if he'd won the Lottery," the Gentleman can always pretend he hasn't asked her out in the first place.

"My mate says that Dave Pugh told him that his sister heard from her friend Jean that Ron Simmons said Specky Jones told him that it was all over the school that Darren Hughes in Year 9 really fancies you, but it's a secret."

Favourite chat-up lines

Robin Hood to Maid Marian: "I bet you I can hit that apple up there, not the big red one there, the little green one way up there, with one arrow... with two arrows... third time lucky... tell you what, bet I can hit the big red one there first shot...."

Juliet to Romeo: "You're to die for."

The Empress of Lilliput to Gulliver: "Hello, big boy."

Van Gogh's girlfriend to Van Gogh: "You've cut off your ear for me! How romantic!"
Van Gogh to girlfriend: "Pardon?"

Queen Guinevere to Sir Lancelot: "Is that a twenty-foot battle lance you're carrying, or are you just pleased to see me?"

Anne Boleyn to Henry VIII: "I could lose my head over you."

Fay Wray to King Kong: "How ya doin', you big ape?"

Lady Hamilton to Lord Nelson: "Hello, sailor."

What Lord Nelson really said to Captain Hardy: "Kiss me, Hardy, but no tongues!"

Peter Pan to Wendy: "You wanna see my Tinkerbell?"

The Eighth Dwarf to Snow White: "Hi, toots. This here's Doc. This is Bashful. These guys are Grumpy, Happy, Sneezy, Sleepy, Dopey...and I'm Horny."

Famous Mancunian chat-up line: "Hey, kid, I'd crawl a thousand miles over broken glass just for one sniff of the smoke from the exhaust pipe of the laundry van carrying your knickers."

Leda to Zeus: "Eh up, mi duck."

WHAT IF YOU FANCY PEOPLE OF YOUR OWN SEX?

During puberty it's usual to be attracted to your own sex. Boys and girls often fancy older students at their school, or perhaps get a crush on one of the teachers. As we grow up, most of us start to fancy people of the opposite sex. This is called being 'heterosexual', from the Greek word *hetero*, meaning other. Some continue to fancy their own sex. This is called being 'homosexual', from the Greek word *homos*, meaning same. *Bi* is the Greek for two. A bisexual is someone of either sex who is attracted to both males and females.

Homosexual men are also known as gays, and women who are homosexual can also be called lesbians or gays. Sexually, they have the same sort of relationships as heterosexuals. They kiss and hug, and use their hands, mouths and sexual organs to give each other pleasure.

SEXUAL AWARENESS

As puberty is all to do with the development of your sex organs, you are soon going to develop desires – including the urge to try out these newly developed bits of your body! The first person you're likely to experiment with is yourself.

Masturbation

During puberty, many girls and boys develop a healthy interest in their genitals. They find that touching and stroking them in a certain way produces sensations that they want to repeat and enjoy. Playing with your genitals is called 'masturbation'.

When a boy masturbates, he usually holds his penis in his fist. It gets bigger and harder as he slides his hand up and down it. When a girl does it, she usually rubs her fingers gently around her clitoris, which gets bigger and harder. Sometimes she may push her fingers up into her vagina. A word of warning to girls, if you push objects into your vagina, you may hurt yourself or cause an infection. Clean fingers are best!

Getting together

Sooner or later, you will feel a sexual curiosity in someone else. It may start with dreams and thoughts about someone you fancy or have a crush on such as a film or pop star. Though you might think this is the only person you could ever fancy, the chances are that your first date will be with somebody quite different. You might want to touch and kiss this person. The first time you do this we bet you'll be feeling half dead with nerves as well as faint with excitement. The good news is that you'll probably feel exactly the same kissing someone for the first time for the rest of your life!

Kissing

Snogging, petting, necking are all names given to sexual kissing and caressing. French kissing (or frenchies or deep kissing) is when mouths open and tongues touch.

When people kiss each other for the first time (and this goes for adults too), they often feel awkward as their teeth crash

together and their spectacles tangle. It might not be as romantic as you'd hoped!

Love bites

A love bite is a whacking yellow brownish bruise that comes up on your skin when your boyfriend or girlfriend sucks it. The neck is a common spot for these strange tokens of affection! *WARNING!* Not everybody appreciates this vampire approach, so ask before you sink your fangs into the neck of a new unsuspecting victim.

Erogenous zones

These are the sexually sensitive areas of the body. They aren't necessarily the same in everybody. When contemplating the delights of the erogenous zones, it's always important to respect the wishes and desires of the person you're with.

Heavy petting and even heavier petting

This is where the erogenous zones swing into action. When you're with someone you're feeling good about, and they feel good about you, there will come a time when you can't resist exploring each other's erogenous zones. Don't attempt to stray into these private places unless your partner wants you to!

It's a very exciting process getting to know the body of someone you care for, so take your time kissing and stroking it. Another reason for taking your time is to avoid getting too involved too soon.

The term 'heavy petting' refers to genital contact that stops short of actual intercourse (see page 90).

What happens when a boy becomes sexually excited?

- *His heartbeat speeds up.*
- *His muscles tense.*
- *His breathing quickens.*
- *His body may get hot and flushed.*
- *His nipples may stand up erect.*
- *His penis erects – it gets harder, bigger and stands out and up from his body.*
- *His testes get bigger.*

What happens when a girl becomes sexually excited?

- *Her heartbeat speeds up.*
- *Her muscles tense.*
- *Her body may get hot and flushed.*
- *Her breathing quickens.*
- *Her breasts may get bigger.*
- *Her nipples may stand up erect.*
- *Her labia swell, getting hot and red.*
- *Her clitoris swells and stands up erect.*
- *Her vagina gets moist.*

ORAL SEX

Of course, heavy petting can't make you pregnant – as long as you take some simple precautions! Be careful that the boy doesn't ejaculate near the girl's vagina in case some sperm finds its way up there. The boy shouldn't even touch her vagina with his penis, as a tiny drop of semen (containing millions of super-energetic sperm!) may seep from its tip. Another way sperm can enter the vagina is if you get semen on your fingers!

Some couples like to lick, kiss and suck each other's genitals. This is very heavy petting indeed. Some like it so much they find it impossible not to orgasm when their partner does it to them! This practice goes by the dignified name of 'oral sex'. As with any other sort of sex, don't try it unless you're both sure you want to. With oral sex it's important to be especially gentle and keep your teeth well out of the way, just using tongues and lips.

Genital hygiene is obviously the first requirement for enjoying oral sex, so before you try it have a wash, a bath or a shower.

And now you definitely need to know about contraception. Read all about it, talk to each other, talk to your doctor or clinic. Decide which method is best for both of you. But whatever you do, don't have full sexual intercourse without it.

CONTRACEPTION

Before you have sex, you need to know how not to make a baby! Though obviously only one of you gets pregnant, both of you need to be mature and take responsibility for making sure it doesn't happen.

Members of some religions are against contraception, believing it to be a sin to stop a new life forming. If you believe this, you will also believe that you should wait until you are married to have sex.

There are several ways of preventing a sperm from fertilizing an egg. 'Barrier methods' physically bar the sperm from entering the uterus, where it could fuse with an egg. The most popular and accessible barrier contraceptive is the condom.

THE CONDOM

The condom is also known as a rubber, a johnny, a sheath, a prophylactic, a durex (after the brand name) or a French letter.

Condoms are tubes designed to fit over the penis. They are made of very fine strong rubber. You buy them in packets from a chemist, and they are usually found near the till, so you don't have to ask for them in a loud booming voice.

When you get home and open the packet, you'll find each condom is sealed in its own hygienic wrapping. Tear one open and you'll find the condom rolled up inside, ready for you to put on. That little bubble at the end is a teat that will catch the sperm when you ejaculate.

It's a good idea to practise using a condom by yourself, before you have sex. First, make your penis

erect! Now place the opening of the condom on the head of your penis and unroll it down the shaft until you reach the base. The little teat stands up at the tip. This will catch the semen.

When you have sex with the condom on, you should take your penis out of your partner's vagina after ejaculation, and remove the condom carefully to prevent spillage. Then throw it away. Don't sling it down the loo or it'll end up on the beach!

There are many good reasons for choosing to use condoms. The condom is a safe method of contraception with no side effects. It is cheap, easily kept in a pocket, wallet or purse, and simple to use. Above all, it protects both partners from sexually transmitted diseases. You might like to ask the girl if she would like to put it on you.

Condoms and safe sex

Condoms are 85 to 98 per cent safe as a contraceptive. They also protect against sexually transmitted diseases For this reason, anyone who is having sex with a new partner should use a condom, even if the woman is on the Pill. Girls should carry condoms as well as boys, so you can always make sex safe.

The female condom

The female condom looks like an unrolled male condom and lines the vagina. It has an inner ring that sits over the cervix (neck of the womb) and an outer ring that lies against the labia. It is made of colourless odourless polyurethane and comes ready lubricated for easy insertion. As with the male condom, the female condom traps the sperm and is removed and thrown away after sex.

Spermicides

Spermicides are creams, jellies, foams or pessaries containing chemicals that kill sperm. They are usually used with barrier contraceptives (condom and cap) as an extra layer of protection, but are not effective if used on their own. You insert them into the vagina before intercourse begins. You can buy spermicides in chemists.

The cap or diaphragm

This is a fine rubber disc on a flexible rim. The girl squeezes it into a boat shape and puts it up inside her vagina. It opens up to fit over the cervix (neck of the womb), where it prevents the sperm from reaching and fertilizing the egg. Caps come in various sizes. They have to be fitted by your doctor or at the family planning clinic, where you will be shown how to insert it yourself. The cap should always be used with a spermicide (see above) smeared around its rim. This combination has been found to be a 95 per cent safe contraception.

AFTER SEX

You will need to leave the cap in place for at least six hours after intercourse, because sperm can live for up to five hours in the vagina. Spermicides are effective for only three hours, so if you make love again after this time, take out the cap and smear it with more spermicide. Don't leave the cap in for longer than 24 hours.

When you remove the cap, wash it carefully with warm soapy water and allow it to dry in a warm place, or pat it dry with a towel.

The sponge

The contraceptive sponge is moistened with spermicide before the girl pushes it up inside her vagina. Neither of you should be able to feel it. You should leave the sponge in for at least six hours after sex, but it can be left in for up to 30 hours. You take it out by hooking your finger round a tape attached to it. The sponge is 75 to 91 per cent effective.

THE PILL

The Pill is a popular form of contraception for those in a steady relationship. It provides 98 to 99 per cent protection against pregnancy and has the advantage over barrier methods that lovemaking can be completely spontaneous. The Pill also regulates the menstrual cycle, reducing heavy bleeding and painful periods, and can be prescribed for this alone. The Pill is available only through a doctor or family planning clinic.

Your doctor or clinic nurse will ask questions about your medical history. If there is heart disease or thrombosis in your family, the Pill is probably not for you, because in some women it can increase the tendency to blood-clotting. Most women have no side effects when taking the Pill, but some experience nausea, headaches, weight gain or depression.

Sometimes there are scare stories about the Pill in the news, but the health risks involved in taking it are slight compared to the risks of unwanted pregnancy and childbirth.

How the Pill works

The full name for the Pill given to women under 35 is 'the combined Pill'. It combines two hormones, oestrogen and progestogen. The Pill keeps the hormone level in your body artificially constant so that ovulation does not occur. Without ovulation, there is of course no egg to get fertilized, so you can't get pregnant.

You take the Pill every day for 21 days, after which you have a seven-day break. During this time, you will have a period.

Packets of Pills are labelled with the days of the week so you can check that you haven't missed a day. Take your Pill at the same time every day – perhaps in the morning when you clean your teeth – to help you remember it. If you remember a forgotten Pill before the next one is due, take it straight away. If you forget a Pill for 12 hours or more, or you have really bad diarrhoea or vomiting, you'll need to use a condom as well for the next 7 days just in case the Pill has not been effective.

OTHER TYPES OF CONTRACEPTION

Experiments are going on all the time to find new methods of contraception. Perhaps in the future there will be a Pill for men. At the moment, the methods described above are the best for young people. However, there are other forms of contraception.

The coil or IUD (intra-uterine device) is a small device made of plastic and copper that is inserted into the womb by a doctor. It must also be taken out by a doctor, but can stay in for up to 5 years. It is 96 to 99 per cent safe. It is usually fitted in older women who have already had children.

Contraceptive hormones can be injected into the body or a device that slow-releases contraceptive hormones can be implanted under the skin.

The rhythm method calculates when the woman is due to ovulate and sex is avoided around that time.

ABORTION

Abortion is an operation that ends pregnancy, and not a form of contraception. In some countries abortion is illegal. In England a girl under the age of 16 has to have her parents' consent to have an abortion.

If you think you could be pregnant, get help straight away. Up to 72 hours after intercourse, your doctor may prescribe the 'morning-after' Pill, a strong dose of hormones that is 99 per cent effective but could make you feel quite rough for a while.

If you miss a period, buy a pregnancy testing kit from the chemist, or take a free test at your doctor's or at a family planning clinic. If the result is positive, you have a right to sympathetic advice.

It can be traumatic to find that you are pregnant. If you decide to have an abortion, do so as soon as possible. Get help with making the decision straight away, not only from your doctor, but from parents, friends and your boyfriend.

Sexual intercourse

There will come a time when you want to have a full sexual relationship. It's a big step to take, so you need to be confident that you're doing the right thing. Sex isn't just about physical excitement – it involves other strong emotions too.

You have to be ready for sex in order to enjoy it – under no circumstances should you be pressured into any sexual activity you don't want.

It's a good idea to ask yourself the following questions:

- **Do you trust the other person? It is terrible to feel let down and betrayed afterwards, and to find out that you were being used.**
- **Are you in the right mood? Listen to your true feelings. Don't have sex just because your friends are doing it and you feel left out.**
- **Have you got adequate contraception? (See pages 85-89.) Don't risk an unwanted pregnancy.**

And talk to your boyfriend honestly about the consequences of having sex.

What happens when you have sex?

To put it clinically, during sexual intercourse the man's penis enters the woman's vagina. Before this happens, the couple excite each other sexually by kissing and caressing. Some people call this foreplay. You'll probably have been doing this together for quite a long time (see Getting together, page 83 and Heavy petting, page 84). Now you're fully equipped with contraception and you've decided to let foreplay lead quite naturally into sex.

So, when both of you are ready and it feels the right thing to do, the man pushes his penis into the woman's vagina. Then he moves his hips so that his penis slides up and down inside it. The woman may also move her hips to increase the feelings of sliding and pushing.

Intercourse usually gets steadily more exciting until either the man or the woman reaches orgasm or 'comes'. This can happen to both partners at once, but it's more likely to happen to first one and then the other.

An orgasm happens when the build-up of excitement and tension is released in a series of powerful muscle spasms that centre on the genitals like shock waves or ripples on a pond. The whole body flushes with heat and may sweat. It tenses, then relaxes. Orgasm lasts only a second or two, but it's a quite blissful feeling.

When a boy comes, he ejaculates (shoots) semen from his penis. Ejaculation is caused when the muscular contractions squeeze sperm out of the testes. The sperm mixes with fluids from the prostate gland and the seminal vesicles, and is propelled at speed down the urethra and out of the body through the tip of the penis.

Intercourse may not last more than a couple of minutes the first time you do it. When you both have more practise it will last much longer.

SOME WORRIES ABOUT FIRST-TIME SEX

First-time sex can be great – but it can also be a disappointment. It's quite natural for nerves and excitement to make you clumsy and awkward. Boys are likely to come very quickly, leaving their partners to wonder what it was all about. For girls, first-time sex can be quite uncomfortable if the hymen is unbroken (see page 30). As the boy's penis pushes through it, there may be a sharp pain and some bleeding. You're not abnormal if you didn't enjoy it much the first time!

It takes a while to get used to someone else's body and to find out what kinds of feelings you and they like. Lovemaking will improve with confidence.

SEX AND THE LAW

Most countries have laws forbidding intercourse under a specific age. This is called the age of consent. In Britain the age of consent is 16 for boys and girls.

IMPORTANT!!!

Condoms are the only protection against STDs.
BOYS – When you have sex make sure you use one.
GIRLS – If you are going to have sex make sure your boyfriend uses one.

SEXUALLY TRANSMITTED DISEASES (STDs)

Diseases that are passed on through sexual contact are called STDs or VDs – venereal diseases. Most are easily cured if you take prompt action in visiting your doctor or special clinic (find the number in the phone book or ask your local hospital). You will usually be given a course of antibiotics. Your partner will also need treatment – if only one of you gets treatment, the infection will recur. Symptoms of an STD are itching or soreness in the genitals or rectum, and there is sometimes a discharge from the vagina or penis. There may also be lumps or rashes near or on the genitals and you can get shooting pains when peeing.

AIDS

What is AIDS?

The letters AIDS stand for Acquired Immune Deficiency Syndrome. AIDS is caused by the human immunodeficiency virus, known as HIV. The HIV virus lives in bodily fluids such as semen and blood. You can get HIV when your body fluids come into contact with those of someone who has HIV already.

What does it do?

Once it is inside the body, the HIV virus invades the white blood cells, which normally fight off disease, then it multiplies and destroys them. As the body's defences are worn down, the AIDS patient catches all sorts of diseases that a healthy body would be able to ward off.

The patient gets weaker and eventually dies from a disease such as pneumonia.

How can it be cured?

There is no known cure for AIDS, but people infected with HIV can often live for many years before they show its effects.

HOW DOES INFECTION OCCUR?

1 HIV can enter the body through a cut with an infected instrument or an injection with an infected needle. This is why drug users are at great risk when they share needles.

2 People can get HIV by having sex with an infected person. A condom provides protection against infection.

HOW CAN I AVOID GETTING AIDS?

- *Always use a condom when having intercourse.*

- *Never share needles used for injecting drugs.*

- *Do not share razors or toothbrushes.*

- *If you are having tattoos or your ears pierced, make sure you see that all the equipment is sterilized.*

SO WHAT'S GOOD ABOUT PUBERTY?

All these problems, so why bother with it?
Is there anything good about puberty?

Try these:

a boyfriend
or girlfriend

- **More privileges**
- **Stay up longer**
- **Becoming independent**
- **Get into (15) films (legally!)**
- **Making decisions**
- **New school**
- **Growing bigger**
- **Getting better at sports**
- **Discovering new experiences**
- **Going to parties on your own**
- **Having a boyfriend or a girlfriend**
- **Getting more money**
- **Getting a job**
- **Feeling more like an adult**
- **Being treated with respect**

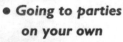

more money

wearing what
you like

going to parties

The list is endless!

There will be some good times and some bad times in your teenage years. But you can make the most of them, whatever they are. Try to like yourself and don't worry if you feel that no one understands you – millions of others are going through puberty thinking exactly the same as you!

Talk to someone about any problems you feel you might have and remember – it will soon be over!

Good luck!

Helplines

Don't suffer in silence — whatever your problem, there is someone you can talk to. All the organizations below have trained counsellors who will give you practical advice and support as well as talking things through. The 0800 numbers mean calls are free from anywhere in Great Britain and Northern Ireland.

CHILDLINE
ℭ (0800) 1111

For children and teenagers. Can discuss any problem — including bullying, sexual abuse, eating disorders. Lines open 24 hours a day.

The NSPCC
(National Society for the Prevention of Cruelty to Children)
ℭ (0800) 800 500

For children and teenagers. Help with any problem but especially sexual or physical abuse. Lines open 24 hours a day, every day.

THE CHILDREN'S LEGAL CENTRE
ℭ (0171) 359 6251

Expert advice on the law and government policies. Lines open between 2 and 5 every weekday.

THE NATIONAL ADVISORY SERVICE ON AIDS
ℭ (0800) 567 123

Leaflet line:
ℭ (0800) 555 777

Advice on AIDS and HIV. Lines open 24 hours a day, every day.

THE TERRENCE HIGGINS TRUST
ℭ (0171) 242 1010

Expert advice on AIDS and HIV. Lines open from midday to 10 pm every day.

THE LESBIAN AND GAY SWITCHBOARD
ℭ (0171) 837 7324

Advice on AIDS and HIV. A chance to chat if you're confused or lonely. Advice on other groups around the country. Lines open 24 hours a day, every day.

BROOK ADVISORY
ℭ (0171) 617 8000

Advice on contraception, pregnancy, abortion and sex-related health problems. Confidential and being under 16 is not a problem. Open 24 hours a day, every day.

THE FAMILY PLANNING ASSOCIATION
ℭ (0171) 636 7866

Advice on contraception, pregnancy, abortions and sex-related health problems. Confidential and being under 16 isn't a problem.

THE BRITISH PREGNANCY ADVISORY SERVICE
ℭ (0171) 222 0985

Counselling and practical advice on abortions. Private clinic so small fees. Confidential and being under 16 is not a problem. Lines open 9 am to 5 pm (7 pm on Tuesdays); 9 am to 2 pm on Saturdays.

EATING DISORDERS ASSOCIATION
ℭ (01603) 621414

Youthline for under 18s
ℭ (01603) 765050

Advice and practical help with bulimia, anorexia nervosa and other eating disorders. Open 9 am to 6.30 pm Monday to Friday; Youthline open 4 pm to 6 pm Monday to Fridays.

TURNING POINT
ℭ (0171) 702 2300

Advice and practical help on drink, drugs and mental health related problems. Open 9 am to 5 pm Monday to Friday.

Index.

A

abortion — 90
acne — 55
AIDS — 93
alcohol — 73
anorexia nervosa — 63
areola — 19, 20

B

birth — 40
blackheads — 54, 55
bras — 22
breasts — 18, 21, 23
bulimia — 63
bullies — 70

C

carbohydrates — 61
castration — 10
cervix — 31, 35
circumcision — 26
clitoris — 29
condoms — 86-7, 92
contraception — 85-9

D

deodorants — 50
diet — 60-3
drugs — 71-7

E

erogenous zones — 84
exercise — 64-5

F

Fallopian tubes — 31, 37, 39, 40
fertilization — 39-40
foreskin — 26, 50

G

genitals — 23-31

H

hair — 11-17, 51
heavy petting — 84
HIV — 93
homosexuality — 82
hormones — 8-10, 19, 36-7, 44-5
hygiene — 49-51
hymen — 29, 30, 92

K

kissing — 83

L

labia — 29
love bites — 83

M

masturbation — 82
menstrual cycle — 33, 36-7, 39
minerals — 61, 62

N

nipples — 19, 20

O

oral sex — 85
orgasm — 91
ovaries — 31, 36-7
ovum — 30, 36-7, 39-40

P

penis — 23-6, 91
periods — 32-9, 42-3, 46
the Pill — 88-9

pregnancy — 40, 90
premenstrual tension (PMT) — 41, 44-5
protein — 61
pubic hair — 12, 13

R

razors — 16

S

sanitary towels — 42-3
scrotum — 27
semen — 39
sex — 39, 78-92
sexually transmitted diseases (STDs) — 92
shaving — 16-17
skin — 54-9
smoking — 72
sperm — 26, 39-40, 91
spots — 53-9

T

tampons — 42, 43, 44
testes — 24, 27
Toxic Shock Syndrome (TSS) — 44

U,

underarm hair — 13
urethra — 27, 29
uterus — 31, 33, 35, 37, 40

V,W

vagina — 29, 31, 35, 40, 91
vitamins — 61, 62
voice, breaking — 5
womb see uterus